*The Body in Crisis*

# Studies in Dance: Theories and Practices

## Series Editorial Board

TITLES IN THE SERIES:

dance
 studies
association

The Dance Studies Association (DSA) advances the field of dance studies through research, publication, performance, and outreach to audiences across the arts, humanities, and social sciences. As a constituent member of the American Council of Learned Societies, DSA holds annual conferences; publishes new scholarship through its book series, proceedings, and Conversations Across the Field of Dance Studies; collaborates regularly with peer institutions in the United States and abroad; and presents yearly awards for exemplary scholarship. A complete list of books in the series can be found on the University of Michigan website, www.press.umich.edu.

# The Body in Crisis

## NEW PATHWAYS AND SHORT CIRCUITS
## IN REPRESENTATION

*Christine Greiner*

Translated by Christopher Larkosh
and Grace Holleran

UNIVERSITY OF MICHIGAN PRESS

ANN ARBOR

For questions or permissions, please contact um.press.perms@umich.edu

Published in the United States of America by the University of Michigan Press
Manufactured in the United States of America
Printed on acid-free paper
First published September 2021

A CIP catalog record for this book is available from the British Library.

*Library of Congress Cataloging-in-Publication data has been applied for.*

ISBN 978-0-472-13245-4 (hardcover: alk. paper)
ISBN 978-0-472-03866-4 (paper: alk. paper)
ISBN 978-0-472-12870-9 (e-book)

Generous support for this translation has been provided by the Dance Studies Association.

*For Francisco*

# Contents

Digital materials related to this title can be found on the Fulcrum platform via the following citable URL: https://doi.org/10.3998/mpub.11883180

# Acknowledgments

It is difficult to say exactly when my interest in the body in a state of crisis arose. It might have been when I started reading Clarice Lispector in my adolescence or reread her work in 1995 during a trip to Japan, or maybe at the turn of the millennium when personal anguish led me to study, with utmost dedication, the philosopher Giorgio Agamben's research on the gray areas between life and death, states of exception, and processes of dehumanization.

Over all these years, the list of interlocutors who helped me understand what makes up this state of crisis got longer and longer. Without them, this book would not exist. Many of them are students turned good friends, such as Claudia Amorim, with whom I have been organizing the collection *Readings of the Body* for Annablume since 2003; Magda Bellini, my partner in studies on blindness and empathy; Marta Soares, who led me to deepen my reading of some of the authors fundamental to the second chapter; Marco Souza, the guardian angel who coordinated the Center of Eastern Studies at the University of São Paulo alongside myself and Cecília Saito, our irreplaceable partner, in addition to the extremely enthusiastic class that attends our study group (Cleide, Marcela, Michiko, Guaxupé, Letícia, Fê, Roberta, Ítala, Ro, Isa, Laís, Lili, Rita, Daniel, and Laurence, among so many others who come and go, circulating both inside Japan and in the surrounding region). I am also particularly grateful to the students (both enrolled and auditing) who attended my Dramaturgy of Dance classes in the Communication of Bodily Arts Program and the Postgraduate Studies Program in Communication and Semiotics in the first semester of 2010, when I finished writing the book and tested many of the ideas that ended up maturing in the classroom.

An event that also marked the beginning of 2010 that had an impact on my final analysis was the fourth edition of *Rumos Dança* (*Dance Directions*) from Itaú Cultural, also in São Paulo. I followed the showings of processes in artistic research alongside choreographers whom I greatly admire (Lia Rodrigues, Alejandro Ahmed, Vera Sala, and Marcelo Evelin) and featured guest André Lepecki. Together, we sparked discussions with other artists and researchers from all over Brazil. I thank you all, especially Sonia Sobral and Cris Espírito Santo for having invited me, as this was one of the first experiences that made me understand the difficulties of collective action to open new fields of possibilities.

I am also very grateful to the folks at the Corpo Rastreado Association and their circle of friends (Gabizinha, Zé Renato, Van, Có, Elaine, and André); to Luis Lois, who invited me to give seminars in his studio, where I truly felt the relationship between art and manifesto; and to the folks at the Centro em Movimento in Lisbon (Sofia, Guida, Mariana, Cristina, Paula, Joana, Graça, and Luz). Our last meeting in 2009, which included Peter Pál Pelbart and Kuniichi Uno, was particularly important to establishing parts of the second and fourth chapters.

During the final revision of this manuscript I also had the valuable opportunity to work for a week in the city of Luís Correia in the northeastern Brazilian state of Piauí, as a guest of *coLABoratório* from the Panorama of Dance in Rio de Janeiro, in partnership with the Dirceu de Teresina Center. This short, intense encounter with young artists and producers once again made me examine what it means to do something together and share all that is uncommon (ideas, ways of life, feelings). In insisting on creating closeness and collective networks of activation, all these experiences of thinking/doing together lead me to believe that it is possible to resist.

Lastly, thank you once again to Helena Katz for the lunches, books, conversations, and valuable suggestions for the final manuscript of this book, which only reaffirmed our partnership of more than twenty years, one that has taught me a great deal about sharing and friendship. In the original 2010 Brazilian edition of the book, I included an article of hers that contextualized a portion of the discussions presented from the theory of *corpomedium*, which we had built together over the previous decade.

# Foreword

Cristina Fernandes Rosa

Brazil has long been a destination for dance scholars and practitioners, from Katherine Dunham to Yvonne Daniel, Barbara Browning, and Pina Bausch. Binding these distinct ventures is the recognition of that geopolitical location as a repository of aesthetic knowledges, including those from Amerindian, European, and African heritages. Conversely, the understanding of Brazilians as producers of knowledge about dance—and the recognition of their scholarship—remains underrated, misconstrued, or otherwise made invisible.

Christine Greiner, a distinguished dance scholar and professor at the Pontifícia Universidade Católica de São Paulo (PUC-SP), is a good example of such a scholarly blind spot. Broadly speaking, Dr. Greiner's research interests concern the political dimensions of communication and bodily arts, though her areas of expertise surround movement practices and body-centered performances from Brazil and Japan. Her prolific record of publications includes articles featured in *The Routledge Companion to Butoh Performance* (2019), *Performance in the Public Sphere* (2018), *Componer el plural: Escena, Cuerpo, Política* (2016), and *Planes of Composition: Dance, Theory, and the Global* (2009), as well as academic journals such as *TDR: The Drama Review, Danza e ricerca: Laboratorio di studi, scritture, visioni, Ebisu: Etudes japonaises*, and *Daruma*. In addition to *O corpo em crise: Novas pistas e o curto-circuito das representações* (2010, translated here), her full-length books include *Fabulações do corpo japonês e seus microativismos* (Fabulations of the Japanese Body and Its Microactivisms, 2017), *Leituras do corpo no Japão e suas diásporas cognitivas* (Readings of the Body in Japan and Its Cognitive Diaporas, 2015), *O corpo: Pistas para estudos indisciplinares* (The Body: Pathways for Interdisciplinary

Studies, 2005), *O Teatro Nô e o Ocidente* (Nō Theater and the West, 2000), and *Butô: Pensamento em evolução* (Butō: Thought in Evolution, 1998). Yet, despite the rigor and relevance of her scholarship, and its impact across Latin America, until now it has remained largely unknown to English-speaking readers.

The translation of Greiner's *O corpo em crise*, a joint effort between the Dance Studies Association's book series Studies in Dance History (SiDH) and the University of Michigan Press, seeks to bridge this gap in the field of dance studies. Despite its compact format, this volume offers a valuable contribution to the critical discussions surrounding bodily arts and their political relevance in the age of neoliberal globalization. Furthermore, this initiative arrives at a critical moment in the development of the performing arts fields. Dance, theater, and performance studies in particular have begun to recognize the ways in which colonial and imperial forces continue to inform the geopolitics of knowledge production in their intersecting areas of studies and, more specifically, to identify lacunae in the scholarly literature produced and consumed across Western/westernized institutions of higher education. In that sense, the translation of Greiner's book may be viewed as a concrete step in the ongoing push for the decolonization of higher education's programs and curricula. As I argued in a book review published in 2011, Greiner's capacity to distill complex ideas and concepts from various fields of inquiry and interweave them in a direct and accessible manner makes this synthetic volume a suitable text for both undergraduate and graduate students. This is, therefore, a useful reference for faculty seeking to decolonize their curricula, giving wider visibility to the scholarship developed in the Global South. The author's unique position as a South American scholar of bodily arts whose research spans East (Japan) and West (Brazil)[1] and the interdisciplinarity of her work, employing approaches from neuroscience, the social sciences, philosophy, and the arts, serve to critically expand current discussions linking biopolitics with theories of corporeality. The translation of *O corpo em crise* will encourage scholars in the performing arts to rethink the role of moving bodies and bodily actions in the political arena. Finally, Greiner's critical attunement to historical and current events across the Global North and South provides new points of departure from which to address a question central to our globalized society: the role and function of alterity within a neoliberal regime of intelligibility that glorifies individualism.

*O corpo em crise* is the sequel to Christine Greiner's monograph *O corpo: Pistas para estudos indisciplinares* (The Body: Pathways for Indisciplinary Studies, 2005), currently in its third edition, republished in Portugal and translated to Spanish. This equally concise and critically acclaimed work offers an introductory overview of the intersection of dance, embodiment, and cognition to those working in the broad area of performing arts. More importantly, it lays out the foundations of a new theoretical approach that Greiner has developed since 2000 in partnership with Dr. Helena Katz, also a professor at PUC-SP, with which to analyze cognitive processes in dance and their political implications (see Greiner 2007 for discussion in English). Titled *corpomídia* (bodymedia), this approach considers bodies as transitory states, constantly exchanging data with the environment, informing and being formed by one another. Yet, contrary to the understanding of bodies as vessels or tabula rasae, they argue that the relationships between bodies and environments "take place through coevolutionary processes that produce a network of perceptual, motor, learning, and emotional preconditions" (Greiner and Katz 2005, 130–31, my translation). And further:

> The body is not a medium through which the information simply passes, because every piece of input information begins a negotiation with the information that is already there. *The body is the result of these interactions, not a place where information is only held.* It is with this notion of media of itself that *corpomídia* deals, not with the idea of media understood as a vehicle of transmission. The media to which the *corpomídia* refers concerns the evolutionary process of selecting information that is constructing the body. (131, my emphasis)

Through *corpomídia* theory, movement is understood as that which enables bodies to act both as articulators of ideas and as articulated media—shaping agents and shaped loci—constantly in flux, in relation to themselves (as processual subjects) and in relation to the (socioeconomic, cultural, political) environments or contexts through which they circulate. Through this theorization, Greiner and Katz have introduced a critically robust body of work that addresses how this relational understanding of subjectivity enables us to better comprehend how apparatuses of power are negotiated at the bodily level, either individually or collectively.

In *O corpo em crise*, published five years later, Greiner departs from *corpomídia* theory to address questions of otherness, positioning that porous approach in dialogue with then-existing scholarship, especially Giorgio Agamben's notion of "state of exception." The question of alterity formation gains a deeper dimension when the author debates the limits of the body in radical scenarios such as warfare settings and military regimes. Examples of what she calls gray areas or *zones of indistinction* include concentration camps, where a collective body is pushed into subhuman conditions, and autocracies, where a sovereign body is granted a limitless use of power over the life of others. Subsequently, she presents a robust network of North-South connections across knowledge production, creative embodiment, and political action. On the one hand, the author gestures toward destabilizing ways of translating self-other relations beyond abyssal dualities. On the other, she points to ways in which the understanding of immunization has pushed the relational construction of subjectivity through exclusionary opposition, or individualism, toward a dangerous and volatile paradigm.

It is perhaps important to note that *O corpo* (2005) and *O corpo em crise* (2010) were written during Brazilian president Luiz Inácio Lula da Silva's two consecutive mandates (2003–10), an era marked by an unprecedented socioeconomic boom and subsequent flourishing of the arts and cultures in the country. During Lula's administration, the government also injected substantial resources into the creation of new state universities with programs in the areas of art production, education, and management. These initiatives were coupled with the implementation of a robust program of scholarships, fellowships, and permanent professorial positions aimed to boost scientific production in all areas of research. Today there are more than forty bachelor's degree programs in dance spread across Brazil as well as two master of arts programs (Universidade Federal da Bahia, UFBA, and Universidade Federal do Rio de Janeiro, UFRJ) and a PhD in dance studies (UFBA), all of which have created a demand for new theoretical models with which to survey and critically analyze the artistic production in the country and generate internationally recognized outputs in the form of original research. Beyond these "official" dance programs, other institutions currently offer accredited interdisciplinary programs that have, in practice, resulted in projects related to the field of critical dance studies. A good example is the bachelor's program in Communication of Bodily Arts (Comunicação das Artes do Corpo) created by Greiner and other colleagues in 1999 at PUC-SP, when she joined that institution as full-time professor, which has in turn contributed to reshaping its master's and doctoral programs. Over the past decades PUC has produced a growing army of scholars and research-artists in the broad area of bodily arts who are both critical of their creative work and active in their scholarly production. Greiner alone has supervised an incredibly large number of master's theses and doctoral dissertations to their successful completion thus far, many of which draw heavily on the groundwork she has developed at the intersection of dance and cognition (in partnership with Helena Katz), in general, and *corpomídia* theory, in particular. All in all, as Greiner reveals, *O corpo em crise* results from the author's various dialogues established with her bachelor's, master's, and doctoral students, several of whom currently occupy professorial positions across the country.

*The Body in Crisis* is divided into three sections: Networks of Destabilization, Operators of Resistance, and Paradigms of Immunization. Part I introduces a blueprint of the field being examined, with chapter 1, "The Agents of the Crisis," departing from postmodern and postcolonial scholarship to identify the exclusionary dichotomy informing the relational construction of the self in modern times, that is, the Platonic-Cartesian body/mind split. It subsequently problematizes the underlying system of organization in which Western/westernized bodies have perceived and represented their relation to the world through segregationist thought and language. To paraphrase Agamben, this embodied mapping includes to exclude. Chapter 2, "Metaphoric Epidemics," expands on Agamben's scholarship, unpacking the link between body and (situated) cognition as well as embodied states of exception and gray areas. Across this chapter, the author lays out three key issues pertaining to the body/medium continuum: the appetite for deterritorialization; the pathologies of the border, after Neil Leach's notion of camouflage (2006); and the insistence on the real, which moves from the hypervisibility of media to the abject.

Part II includes chapters 3 and 4, "Principles of Experience" and "Circuits of Activation." The former examines how perception (as a cognitive action), mirror neurons, and affect influence the situated knowledge we construct of others. Greiner implicates the body—understood as *corpomídia*—in the production of meaning. Meanwhile, chapter 4 departs from Karl Marx's notion of "immaterial labor" to consider how movement shapes thinking patterns and how the materiality of the body can be mobilized for political action. In part III, chapter 5, "Systemic Crises," dives deeper into the central puzzle associated with self-other relations, that is, the *immunization paradigm*. While approximation, mimicry, consumption, and exposure can be seen as steps toward the translation of the other, as the previous chapters convey, the affirmation of one's identity activates mechanisms of resistance against the threat of "contamination."

Ultimately, Greiner argues, while immunization may function as a form of political resistance, by inhibiting one's ability to engage or empathize with others, it can also put the sustainability of communities at risk.

Though this book was written a decade ago, the discussions Greiner presents are astonishingly relevant to today's affairs worldwide. Her theorization of the immunization paradigm, in particular, speaks directly to a number of events informing our global context—from the genocide of Indigenous population of Brazil to the refugee crisis in Europe, Donald Trump's wall on the US-Mexico border, Brexit, and the "anti-" Citizenship Amendment Act in India— and, subsequently, works of arts that have sprung from them. Meanwhile, the crisis that Greiner reveals in the following pages is not a cause for despair but rather an opportunity. Otherness, as she argues in more recent publications, may also be viewed as a creative state, for discourses might be fixed, but bodies are always already engaged in processes of transformation.

London, December 2019

# Translators' Note

## Christopher Larkosh and Grace Holleran

As is often said jokingly, in reference to Renée Zellweger's famous line in *Jerry Maguire*,[1] the 1996 Hollywood film of the same generation as many of those cited in this work, this book "had us at hello." Beginning with the engaging title of the acknowledgments in the Portuguese text—*redes de afeto* (networks of affection)— Christine Greiner articulates the warm relationship she has cultivated over the years with a large network of colleagues, students, and other fellow travelers in her interdisciplinary field or dance space. This work seemed to embrace others from the start; it was almost as if space has been left for us here.

Greiner also makes clear from the outset that the book departs from the work of two prominent twentieth-century Brazilian authors: both the Concrete poet and translation theorist Haroldo de Campos, already a key reference in this context for his theorization on translation as *transcreation*, and the novelist and short story writer Clarice Lispector, whose *A paixão segundo G.H.* (The Passion According to G.H.) and *Um sopro de vida* (A Breath of Life) Greiner reread while in Japan. The renewed attention given to Lispector in 2020, the centennial of her birth, as perhaps one of Brazil's greatest contributors to world literature was another reason why this book appeared to be an ideal translation project for us, as was the way Greiner places the act of translation front and center before a broad landscape of global references in the interest of rethinking and dismantling the traditional mind/body binary.

Moreover, as this book was originally intended for use by students of literary and critical theory, we both—as a professor and student of contemporary Brazilian literature and culture as well as Portuguese-English translation—had a particular vested interest in seeing this book become a reality in English, both for ourselves and for our students in literary theory and translation theory, now and in the future. This translation is the result of one such collaboration between teacher and student as part of a directed study in advanced academic translation.

We inscribe this English-language edition under the rubric of what might be called gender-sensitive and embodied translation. But what does that really mean in practical terms? Is this a queer translation? A feminist one? Our answer, in a word, is yes: as Greiner's work fundamentally deconstructs the mind/body binary, we find that queerness, too, departs from a political responsibility to critically dissolve binaries and barriers; third-wave and other contemporary feminisms also see gender through a non-binary lens. For this reason, we strove in our translation to subvert the conventional usage of *o homem* (man) as a synonym for humans, here usually transposing it in this way, that is, into the plural.

In our continued effort to deconstruct the boundaries between different languages and different works, we frequently cross-checked our translation with original works and other translators' texts in order to translate the rich vocabulary Greiner cites from various theorists. For example, Peter Sloterdijk's translation of Friedrich Nietzsche, subsequently retranslated by Greiner, left us at a loss as to which language to begin from. While still consulting Greiner's Portuguese text, we opted to work from Nietzsche's 1884 German original as well.[2]

When faced with Giorgio Agamben's conceptualization of *la vita nuda*, derived from the ancient Greek zoë, we had to negotiate with the fact that the term seemed to morph in different contexts. While the Italian can be translated fairly directly into Portuguese as *a vida nua*, we wrestled with several interpretations in English: "bare life," "naked life," "life in the rough/raw," and "life, pure and simple," to name a few. In the end, we opted to use "bare life" consistently in our translation, due to its proliferation in English translations of Agamben and to allow the reader more facility in tracing the term's various appearances in the book. We leave these other possible options here for you to consider.

Conversely, the Portuguese *dispositivo* necessitated various English interpretations throughout the text. In general usage, it is commonly translated as "device," but because unique theoretical complexities are introduced with each new discussion of the concept, we chose to adapt our translations based on previous English renderings of the cited philosophers. There is no consensus among translators, of course, but we found Agamben's "apparatus" to be most appropriate for Foucault's *dispositif*. In passages referencing Gilles Deleuze and Félix Guattari, we substituted "apparatus" with Brian Massumi's translation "assemblage" (from *agencement*), in order to illustrate the philosophers' simultaneous inspiration from and reimagining of Foucault. In a few uses outside of the immediate context of a specific philosopher, we opted for "device." We hope these remarks give the reader a more complete picture of the diverse ways of thinking these pivotal concepts represent for Greiner.

We also wish to offer our experiences with the metaphorics of translation. Greiner's text reveals a rich conceptual landscape of translation in the context of neuroscience, modern and contemporary intellectual history, and recent developments in dance and other visual and performing arts, a landscape on which we could plot out possible mappings for an eventual translation of the text itself. For example, the author's discussion of mirror neurons represents a possible quantum leap in how we think about the embodied nature of all acts of translation as neurological mimicry that extends beyond the limits of any medium, including the mind itself. In approaching the text in this way, we found our own role as translators similarly metaphorized, becoming a sort of agent operating between disciplinary idioms, languages, cultures, and other specialized and generalized forms of embodied communication, with Agamben and Primo Levi providing here the most poignant and extreme examples of how this practice is interpreted and represented in intellectual history and culture.

Finally, our own *rede de afetos*: we work as a team of two minds, but also two sets of hands, two sets of eyes, and two different bodies in crisis. We also operate from distinct forms of intellectual awareness before the concepts presented in this book. Our process was cultivated by a relationship of *cura*, a word that in Portuguese and a few other Romance languages means caring, curing, and curating, and has been perhaps the most significant operative metaphor for us as cotranslators. In other words, we simply did our best work for each other, keeping healthy boundaries while reaffirming a sense of empathy (a concept discussed in depth in this book), understanding, and related commitment to work alongside each other. This complex pedagogical juxtaposition was further complicated by the COVID-19 pandemic, and the seemingly endless summer (June–September 2020) during which this translation was both begun and completed—one in which we never, throughout this entire embodied cotranslational process, were able to meet up in person.

We are grateful for the chance to work together in the PhD Program in Luso-Afro-Brazilian Studies and Theory at the University of Massachusetts Dartmouth, and for the unique conversational space that our spring 2020 graduate seminar Lusodiasporic Contemporaneities provided us: one which also, oddly enough, unwittingly prepared us to continue making connections between the readings assigned and discussed in the course (Marx, Freud, Saussure, Barthes, Lacan, Adorno, Arendt, Deleuze and Guattari, Derrida, Kristeva, Žižek, and more) for our eventual work together on this text. This course continued, even as the pandemic would eventually intervene to remove us from the physical space, replacing it with a hardly comparable cybernetic and virtual space, another seemingly irreversible paradigmatic shift. And yet the resulting shift in thinking also seemed to prefigure and inform, in some uncanny way, our translations of the discussions raised in *The Body in Crisis*: ones of illness, immunization, and, above all, epidemics and their metaphors.

Out of these separate yet overlapping spaces of pedagogy, research, and now cotranslation, we wish to acknowledge editor LeAnn Fields at the University of Michigan Press, and Professor Cristina Fernandes Rosa at Roehampton University for their faith in us as cotranslators and their patience as we completed our assignment.

Finally, our sincere thanks to the author herself, for writing such a profoundly timely and transformative text in Portuguese on the body, one that engages so intensely the practical act of translation as guiding concept. Here, translation is not just a means to transmit ideas across linguistic boundaries; it is a political act that calls those very boundaries into crisis, much as the bodies on either side of them—whether those bodies are of translators, migrants, or dancers—leap here and there, back and forth and in all directions, between opposites and neutral zones, neither here nor there, perhaps on the edge, but always somewhere in between.

East Providence, Rhode Island and
Bridgeport, Connecticut
September 2020

## Postscript to the Translators' Note

Christopher Larkosh, professor of Portuguese at the University of Massachusetts Dartmouth and cotranslator of this text, passed away suddenly in his home in East Providence, Rhode Island on December 24, 2020, just months after we finished our translation. It is hard to know how to proceed in the wake of such a tremendous loss.

A force to be reckoned with in the fields of comparative cultures and literatures, literary and cultural theory, translation, gender studies, and multilingualism, Chris was a person who felt deeply, and this was apparent in everything he did. He was always aware of his positionality and in tune with the world around him, even when that world was hostile. Nothing was purely academic for Chris, so our collaboration was never just about completing assignments. We spoke frequently of navigating our new world of isolation and virtuality, of the collective crisis we faced as we translated *The Body in Crisis*. His work was fueled by passion with a zeal for social justice, always on the side of those most marginalized by society. His remarkable intellect and talent left a lasting mark on everyone who knew him.

Chris's connection to Christine Greiner's work radiates in the following translation and in our collaborative process of crafting it—and it is precisely this kind of connection that Chris brought to everyone he encountered in his travels. My hope is that as this text circulates through the various fields of research it engages with, Chris's legacy will live on in the scholars and students who follow in his tireless work.

Grace Holleran
January 2021

# Preface to the English Edition

Christine Greiner

This book was originally published in Portuguese in 2010 by the publishing house Annablume in São Paulo. The idea to translate it into English came a decade later from Professor Cristina Fernandes Rosa at Roehampton University in England. Although she is Brazilian, Rosa has been researching and working between the United States and the United Kingdom for many years, which makes her the ideal reader (and interlocutor) for this research, given that in order to think/feel what I am calling "the body in crisis" it is important to inhabit a certain flux, experiencing different perspectives and points of view. With that in mind, I wish to express my profound gratitude to Professor Rosa, as well as to the University of Michigan Press, especially LeAnn Fields, for supervising the process of getting this manuscript translated and republished in English. Suggestions of the dance historian and dramaturg Clare Croft, also from the University of Michigan, were also very important in the completion of the book's presentation. Finally, I would like to thank the translators Christopher Larkosh and Grace Holleran, who did much more than just translate the text into English, becoming accomplices to my research.

Rereading the book again so many years later, I realized that although I had published other titles in the following years, the topic of crisis—and more specifically, that crisis generated by the difficulties of dealing with alterity—continued to be absolutely fundamental, both in my own personal studies and in the political context in which we live. Here I am referring not only to Brazil, but to so many other countries overwhelmed by the same conservative, moralist, and neoliberal wave that makes it difficult to relate to anything that seems different from the models given a priori and from identity politics.

Not without reason, debates on gender, racism, colonialism, and decolonization have assumed greater importance over the last decade. Authors who were unknown in Brazil until quite recently, such as the Cameroonian author Achille Mbembe; the exponents of Black studies in the United States such as Fred Moten, Tavia Nyong'o, and Saidiya Hartman; the poet Audre Lorde; and irreverent writers in queer studies including the Spaniard Paul B. Preciado, the French Virginie Despentes, the US American Jack Halberstam, the Chinese Xiang Zairong, and so many others, brought new perspectives to the discussion on the multiplicity of possible ways of life. Such thinkers may not have directly influenced research in Brazil, but they nourished us with myriad ideas and sentiments, opening the possibility for encounters with our own experiences and singular narratives. So it is all about another kind of movement. Instead of adopting foreign authors as if we were followers of their proposals (victimized by colonialism), what I'm witnessing most recently in research and creative processes from professors and artists in Brazil is an encounter with and an empathy for a set of questions that reverberate in some international bibliographies such as those I have cited before and so many others that appear over the course of the book. In other words, what is of greatest interest to us is when thinkers such as these question the assemblages of power that overwhelm us.[1] Some are in Central Europe and North America, but still offer a critical perspective regarding their own contexts. Others, much like us in Brazil, observe and propose different geopolitical perspectives that, in turn, nurture other ways of understanding life, producing their research/artistic creations on the African continent, in Asia, and across Latin America.

Starting out from these bibliographies and their reverberations among us, I became more and more interested in the crossings between academic writing and fiction, philosophical essays and poetic writing, along with what are called fabulations. The term *fabulation* has been used in different ways and traditionally refers to literature with a unique capacity to deal with fiction as a power to generate movements. In some ways, as Tavia Nyong'o observes, fabulation creates a deconstructive relationship between history and script, recognizing the inevitability of imagination in time, as Henri Bergson first pointed out, followed soon after by Gilles Deleuze, to contemplate the creative nexus between time and memory.

Nyong'o, however, is interested in a unique angle of fabulation related to the appearance of worlds in the telling of tales that were not made to survive. In this sense, Afro-fabulation—which is the specific topic of his research—can be seen as the persistent reappearance of what was never meant to appear (or can never appear), what was covered up the whole time by other forms of representation, in the range of possibility of quasi-representations and never as an existing one.

In this sense, fabulation has nothing to do with lying, as is commonly thought. To tell a tale, from this political angle, is to expose the relationship between truth and lies in other ways of meaning, and not just those subservient to moral judgments and ideologies (like those propagated, for example, in what we now call fake news). The concept of Afro-fabulations is thus closer to the critical fabulation of the feminist historian Saidiya Hartman,[2] used to critique the erasures and silencing over the course of history, and to the speculative fabulation of Donna Haraway,[3] who proposes opening new pathways in order to project bodies, narratives, and worlds. Although the questions that motivate these authors are not always identical, one thing they have in common is how telling stories is one way of making explicit those histories covered up by politics and assemblages of domination.

One may come to the conclusion, once again, that fabulation does not camouflage truth, but looks for ways to expose it through fictional strategies such as poetry, theater, and performance.

At the same time that I sought to draw closer to those narratives that were not part of my research when I wrote this book, I also continued to go deeper into what I began to call somatic fabulation and otherness as a state of creation. With this in mind, I continued to follow the research of the neuroscientist António Damásio, who had already been quoted and discussed at length in this book, and built a number of bridges with the Japanese researchers Shigenori Nagatomo and Yasuo Yuasa. More than ever before, I reinforced the hypothesis that alterity can be a state of creation when crisis and failure cease to be understood as something to be made up for or corrected, and instead find their power precisely in what escapes from both the models given a priori and normalized life.

My challenge has been to recognize these fabulations through the movements of bodies as more than just literary narratives and dramaturgical experiments. Starting from the arts of the body (dance, theater, and performance), they do not simply illustrate the political debates proposed by discursive practices, but also present alternative proposals themselves. Giorgio Agamben—a significant point of reference for my research on the body in crisis—has also reflected on artistic creation and its political role, acknowledging that artistic practice is what makes life a life-form, which is, in turn, an act of resistance.[4] Inspired by the *Abécédaire* (Alphabet) of Gilles Deleuze,[5] Agamben confirms that the act of resisting is a form of liberation from those who hold power over life.

Ultimately, bodies in crisis are nothing more than living bodies. They are errant bodies that create in order to breathe and open pathways that continue beyond dichotomies, whether they are body-mind, nature-culture, self-other, subject-object, East-West, North-South, or so on.

The recognition that *The Body in Crisis* is still timely ten years later provokes ambivalent feelings. On one hand, it brings to light the radicalization of certain situations in which Agamben's thanatopolitics and Mbembe's necropolitics seem to establish even more profound fissures; at the same time, it exposes the irreversible movements of artistic and social resistance that seek to provide evidence for colonial traces, the acts of silencing, and the omissions with which we are always living.

It is crucial at this moment in time to acknowledge that the visibility of these abuses and their respective productions of death have set up new possibilities for action and decision that deepen the crisis in order to face new specters that may awe or frighten us. By confronting these specters we can activate new movements and breakthroughs in life.

São Paulo, December 2019

# Introduction

A history of affects and losses permeates this book. In a way, it is a continuation of the book *O corpo: Pistas para estudos indisciplinares* (*The Body: Pathways for Indisciplinary Studies*, 2005), but it also reveals a preoccupation with personal experiences.

Its purpose is to examine connections between the thinking of a number of authors in the areas of political philosophy, communication, the arts, and cognitive sciences, in order to give greater visibility to radical experiences that question the limits of the body, as is the case with states of exception, involuntary nomadisms, acts of inclusion in order to exclude, symbolic cannibalisms, and the banalization of everyday evils. In terms of processes of artistic creation, particularly important are those experiences that insist on defying the rules of employability and established aesthetic models.

I will analyze four circuits of activation: the agents of the crisis, metaphoric epidemics, fields of destabilization, and operators of resistance.

The main areas of risk appear right away, marked by the precariousness of their representations and by the insistence on the real as a contingency and an attribute of life. As Giorgio Agamben (2008) notes, the contemporary is that which does not adhere to its own time, but instead always seeks a distance from it, a certain obscurity. Without this, it would not be possible to maintain a critical stance.

It is not an easy task to transit through these unnamed and often imperceptible chasms. All of it, including the analysis of works and discourses, seems insufficient. The urgency lies in recognizing different forms of life. In the end, that is what this book is about: dimly lit experiences, without a voice. Sometimes they happen in the depths of the body, sometimes in the world, dripping down its edges.

## PART I

# Networks of Destabilization

Those who speak from scars establish silence.

  (from Juliano Pessanha to Nietzsche)

A unique and shared world awaits the awakened, but those who stay in bed turn inward to their own worlds.

  (Heraclitus cited by Giorgio Agamben)

# 1

# The Agents of the Crisis

## *The Precarious Nature of Translations*

Haroldo de Campos has said that the translator is first and foremost a transcreator. In this context, nothing is literal or absolute. That which seems unspeakable by language can always be translated as a desire to say. There is a secret speech in silence that causes translation to approximate creation, in addition to dealing necessarily with some kind of alterity. That's what makes it so complex.

As a semiotician and a reader of Max Bense, Campos understood information as a process of signs with a certain degree of order. However, he differentiated between documentary information relative to something observable; the semantic information that accentuates something not necessarily observable (such as a value judgment); and aesthetic information, which operates in the realm of the unpredictability and improbability of signic classification, codified by the very form transmitted by the artist, inseparable from its fulfillment.

The notion of translation as transcreation has not become obsolete; it has, however, gained an ever-more explicit political character. To say that cultural translation is the differential task of anthropology and semiotics has become cliché. The question at hand is how the operation can be carried out successfully. To start, a "good translation" would ideally be efficient in deforming and subverting the translator's conceptual devices in order to transform the target language or way of thinking, but it doesn't always work that way. Martin Heidegger believed that it was only possible to translate a word if the translator was driven by the thought that necessitated the word, that is, by the horizon of experience based on what the word enunciated. That is why translation so often seems impossible, generating nothing more than "seeing the self in the other."

From a political perspective, and with all the difficulties that revolve around relations of alterity, I identify at least four strategies that characterize the different steps of translation, cultivating relatively stable levels of transformation: approximation (communication with the Other), imitation (which can reflect the fetish for the Other), devouring (appropriation of the Other), and exposition (opening to the Other).

These phases are not at all sequential and constantly intermingle. They are always marked by a certain "improbability of signic classification," giving new shape and dimension to "aesthetic information" (or that which presents the sensitive nature of processes) at an inflection point for each and every translation.

After World War II, due to the geopolitical reorganization of the world and the difficulties involved in this process, "translating" became a primary operation of survival, no longer solely of interest to professional poets and translators. Translation, as with the formulation of theories (which can also be understood as a kind of translation), became admittedly provisory, accidental, discontinuous, and dependent on a state of dynamic relations. Perhaps it has always been that way, and what changed is that a few radical situations made the issue of fragility and untranslatability explicit outside of aesthetic experiences, permeating each and every inter- or transcultural translation.

For anyone interested in the topic, there are important sources in the vast mapping of François Dosse (*Histoire du structuralisme*, volumes 1 and 2, 1991–92), which outlines the trajectory of discussions and reflections to this end. The author classifies structuralism as a methodological alternative that comprehensively encompassed the social sciences and left lasting marks on all fields of study in the so-called humanities. It has a basic chronology and many intersections (cultural, temporal, etc.). To this day, in Brazil and elsewhere, a number of studies represent radical changes in ways of understanding coexistence and its possibilities of communication and translation, such as Heidegger's existential analysis, Maurice Merleau-Ponty's phenomenology of corporality, Michel Foucault's microphysics of powers, and Jacques Derrida's exercises of deconstruction.

The starting point that marks the proliferation of this research, Dosse explains, was *Cours de Linguistique Générale* by Ferdinand Saussure, published in 1916 and recontextualized by anthropology, especially through the works of Claude Lévi-Strauss (*Les structures élémentaires de la parenté*, 1952, and *Anthropologie structurale*, 1958). This is because these books targeted new procedures of descriptive research and analysis, which had up to that point been predominant in anthropology, replacing them with structural analysis. A new way of relating with the world was emerging, one much broader than those restricted to a single specific method.

From this moment on, a number of events unfolded. The study of forms and relations (instead of substances and qualities) was always in the foreground, but formulations varied greatly, generating diverse strategies, such as Lévi-Strauss's binary oppositions, the semiotic framing of Algirdas Julien Greimas, and the linguistic games proposed by Jacques Lacan. It is not pertinent to explain each one of these strategies here, but it is important to observe that all these authors agreed that it was indispensable to deal with a not-necessarily-visible reality that could be translated in different ways. Some examples include Lacan's structural unconscious, Greimas's deep structure, Lévi-Strauss's canonical formula of myths in, and the episteme in Foucault. In this sense, the work *Les mots et les choses* (The Order of Things), written by Foucault in 1966, clarifies that discourse served both to mask reality and to translate it.

There are those who say that the structuralist attitude installed a kind of "philosophy of distrust" for questioning the supremacy of large subjects, the cult of Jean-Paul Sartre's existentialism, and the preeminence of reason—and for good reason.[1]

In addition to the authors cited, Roland Barthes stood out in the first generation of the movement, with a new literary theory and the passage from symbolic consciousness to pragmatic consciousness, which accentuated the awareness of the ever-present paradox in living phenomena. Barthes, Gérard Genette, Tzvetan Todorov, and Michel Serres were considered some of the most important representatives of semiological structuralism, whereas Louis Althusser, Pierre Bourdieu, Foucault, Derrida, and Jean-Pierre Vernant founded so-called historicized or epistemic structuralism.

Until 1966, these movements spread in full force to discuss, above all, the possibility of translating signic structures. But, starting in 1967, many critiques of this school of epistemology proliferated, and the movement began to be considered an expression of an abusive formalism. This discontent radicalized with the political movements of May 1968, leading Foucault, Althusser, Barthes, Lacan, and Lévi-Strauss to assume a certain amount of critical distance.

At this time, the majority of the authors who had marked the first generation of structuralism had already died, including many of those responsible for the most revolutionary branch of the movement.[2] Here new orientations emerged, grouped under the category of poststructuralism, which had to do with the valorization of thought-action and relationships between the individual and the political. The subject of historicity replaced the subject of structure, and the notion of translation transformed into a type of systemic translation that combined simultaneous processes in diverse levels of description and temporalities, supported by the relationships between body and environment.

During this period, there was a displacement from cognitive sciences and political philosophy to studies of the conscious based on pragmatic research. In other words, it was not a matter of "unveiling" the unconscious as a point of departure, but turning it into a point of arrival, without distancing reason from emotion, or conscious from unconscious.[3] The social sciences started to respond to a possible humanism without the Enlightenment vectors that had characterized the understanding of history up until this point, centering on ideal models of an orderly world.

In this context, three thinkers were instrumental in making the transition to so-called posthistory: Friedrich Nietzsche (1844–1900), Charles Darwin (1809–82), and Martin Heidegger (1889–1976).

The references to Nietzsche are the most explicit. Derrida even claimed that during a 1967 car ride that he spent with Foucault, the latter confirmed the already well-known importance of Nietzsche in his work and justified the omission of Heidegger, whom he found to be "incredibly important, incredibly difficult and . . . out of his scope." The fact is, implicitly or explicitly, both Nietzsche and Heidegger inspired an entire generation of thinkers and are often cited to this day. One of the principal reasons is that language was always a fundamental field of study to them both. It could be said that the two indirectly collaborated on the characterization of structuralism that reached its peak by generalizing the linguistic model to include the entire field of knowledge of the human sciences. However, that doesn't mean that their theories have been "applied" in a servile sense or that they shared similarities. In reality, their ideas of language were quite different and can be better perceived in the multiplicity of deployment that they fertilized in their evolutionary processes.

Between 1873 and 1874, Nietzsche demonstrated the problems with the supremacy of Western history in *Unzeitgemässe Betrachtungen* (Untimely Considerations), defending pluralistic values, places, and presents. It was also during this time that Darwin introduced his theory, overturning the creationist and anthropocentric perspective that had until then been enforced to explain the origin of the human species. Nietzsche opposes the Enlightenment ideas that had already been destabilized by the recognition that Earth was not the center of the universe, nor humans the center of living beings, and, in his own way, Heidegger takes up some Nietzschean questions in order to critique modernity. But the most relevant point is that it became increasingly clear that the notion of progress had no place in the scope of history.

Heidegger sought the house of being in language, in the hope that he could discover how to live in this "place." The desire for power as sensed in being would result in an occurrence that he called *Dasein*. This term was translated as the human presence or being, the being-in-the-world, whose fundamental elements were, according to Zeljko Loparic (2004), personal identity, the world, and the inhabitance of the world. For Heidegger, this being-in-the-world was a being-towards-death, because one day, inevitably, it would cease to be-in-the-world. "Da" in *Dasein* means here or there; in other words, it represents an opening to spatiality. But this was not to say that the environment is what sheltered the enigma of the human being, as is the case with other living beings. Heidegger created a clear differentiation. Living beings cease to live, but only humans die. The human being's residence is language, unlike other living beings. In his work, language is also not confused with voice. Thus, the experience of being is the experience of a voice that calls without speaking. Human thought and word are born as an echo of that voice and go to the limit in which the silent experience of this having-place of language in voice and in death is realized. To understand these relations proposed by Heidegger is to dive into his constitutive negativity, as Giorgio Agamben explained in his seminars about language and death (2006).[4]

Nietzsche, in turn, insists on the importance of a type of ear to which his work is directed and which, in a way, feeds Heideggerian reflection in order to draw attention to "desertification." Nietzsche's expression "the desert grows" illuminates and intrigues Heidegger because the desert, in this case, is not erosion or deforestation, but the banishment of necessity, memory, and time. Nietzsche's thought always demanded another type of understanding, based on more than just rational comprehension. His philosophical gesture was not reduced to the content that reason is apt to preserve, but invites one to listen to sensitive perception. It values the fact of both being and not being understood. *Thus Spoke Zarathustra* (1883–85) is a book for everyone and no one. Nietzsche was partisan to the dissolution of the category of the new (as something unprecedented) while having been, himself, absolutely an innovator. As Peter Pál Pelbart (2003) suggests, he was the "dawn of counterculture" and could even be considered the "archenemy of postmodernism," who ended up taming pillars of modern culture like Karl Marx and Sigmund Freud. In terms of history, he was the thinker of the end of history, like Heidegger, who sought the history of being that was nothing but a history without history, without feeling, without affiliation, without periodization. One of his beautiful metaphors was a blooming a rosebush in the spring sprouting many buds, but without a trunk, without roots. A fragmented history was announced, without a subject to make sense of any historical development.

In stating that God was dead, Nietzsche also did away with the reference to immutable human nature and, opposing humanism as a doctrine, negated any theory that attributed to humans the central role of subject as full being. Peter Sloterdijk, in his polemic conference *Rules for the Human Zoo: A Response to Heidegger's Letter on Humanism* (1999), attributes the communitarian fantasy underlying all humanism to the model of a literary society in which the participants discover, through reading the canon, a sort of common love for "inspiring messages." This is because the nucleus of humanism, Sloterdijk explains, is always the fantasy of a cult or club of those who were elected to "know how to read." To the Old World and to modern nation-states, knowing how to read meant participating in a mysterious elite. Not by coincidence, the knowledge of grammar generated the word *glamour*, which originally meant bewitchment or occult knowledge. The bourgeois humanism that comes next is no more than the power to impose the classics and claim the universal value of national readings. Evidently, it is not about a determinist relationship between the classical past and modernity, but a degree of efficient adaptability that cultivated the triad of power-knowledge-speech in diverse contexts.

The impact of all this among thinkers who discussed political philosophy and new conceptions for constructing and documenting history is enormous. For Foucault, the choice not to apprehend the continuities that announce the world by enunciating it is clearly Nietzschean inspired. On the contrary, he is interested in the discontinuities and oscillations of the episteme. His preference for genealogy is justified in that the genealogist needs history to "conjure the chimera of origin and not to canonize it" (Foucault 1971, 150).[5]

Beyond the death of God, Nietzsche also announced the disintegration of the human face. Departing from this statement, Foucault (1966, 396–97) opened up other dilemmas (both implicitly and explicitly): How to translate a man without a face? How to elaborate a critical discourse in the new approaches to temporality? How to survive without the notions of identity and truth?

These topics were intimately related to the new modes of coexistence and to the difficulties maintaining a certain distance that would make understanding oneself possible, starting from other perspectives. Boaventura de Sousa Santos (2000) reminds us that theories never reduce reality to what exists; rather, they create a field of possibilities and evaluate nature and the alternatives in their surroundings in relation to what is empirically given. In this way, they deal with the same difficulties all the time.

Constructing a critical theory is not only "criticizing," but relating what exists and is empirically observable to something that is a possibility and cannot be considered a given. In this sense, it can be concluded without much controversy that not all translation formulates a theory, but that all theory is a type of translation (of other theories, of other cultures, of bodily states, and so on).

To further develop the discussion, Sousa Santos does not provide a critical survey of structuralist or poststucturalist theories, preferring to address the passage from the postmodern to the postcolonial and from there to continue on beyond one or the other, in order to avoid paralyzing his reflection within categories given a priori.

Because of the political connotations that these terms represent, it seems increasingly crucial to try out other possible formulations. The debate around postmodernity began in the 1980s. Typically, the term referred to the exhaustion of scientific paradigms supported by models of rationality that made a distinction between subject and object, nature and culture, or nature and society. A conception of reality was sought that was no longer dominated by a deterministic ideology of mechanization, or by the idea of "truth" as a transparent representation of reality. At the time, the postmodernist debate still seemed to invigorate a separation between scientific knowledge and all other forms of knowledge; simultaneously one witnessed a gradual implosion of those fractures. The context was one of decentralization, and this central objective was supported by the displacement of European culture, the deconstruction of metaphysics, and the emergence of an ethnological consciousness to replace historical consciousness.

Many Western intellectuals began to interrogate their own antipodes, which didn't necessarily need to be faraway peoples (in the East, for example), but simply different ways of being, exposing tensions between presence and absence. The enunciation of cultural difference problematized the binary division of past and present, tradition and modernity, as much on the level of cultural representation as on that of its legitimate interpellation. The presence of a third space, as Homi Bhabha (2003) proposed, becomes the necessary condition for the articulation of cultural difference. The in-between space, Bhabha says, charges the signifying bundle of culture, avoiding the politics of polarity and allowing others to emerge out of ourselves. That is because, until then, the Other had been seen more as a horizon of difference than as an agent of articulation and diversity. Even when intellectuals were engaging in serious research (the Japan of Barthes, the China of Julia Kristeva, the Nambikwara of Derrida, the Turkish despot of Montesquieu), the Other always appeared in a relationship of domination, mystification, or admiration.

In the 1990s, the crisis of capitalism and socialism, mainly in Eastern Europe, broadened the concept of the postmodern because, apart from the wearing down of the aforementioned paradigms, other questions of an epistemological, political, and social nature began to emerge. The geopolitical order of the world was destabilized. The prefix *post-* became an increasingly problematic term, suggesting a temporal sequence and a denial. Curiously enough, the changes of the 1980s did not seem so universal, and were centered in the societies where modernity had been achieved most effectively. When understood as a critique of modern reason, postmodernity seemed quite different in those countries that had hardly organized a clear idea of modernity. The appropriation of the same vocabulary to refer to different situations seemed like a trap, which transformed the idea of emancipation of society into a new form of social oppression. The modern values of equality, freedom, and solidarity remained relevant, but at the same time, in societies with modern problems that arose from these values not being realized, the disparities became all the more glaring. With the establishment of mass media culture in the so-called First World in 1918 (broadcast radio), after 1945 (television), and subsequently with the internet, human coexistence in present-day society was reestablished on a different basis. As Sloterdijk explains, there are doors left wide open for postliterary, postepistolary, and posthumanist situations. These refer precisely to the flow of information and of people that began to transit through the margins. So it's not a stretch to acknowledge that the era of modern humanism as a model for school and professional training ended, once one gives up the illusion that overarching political and economic structures are organized out of some model of friendship and solidarity. The underlying topic of humanism has always been the uplifting of humans out of their often brutal existence, but its thesis persisted: good readings lead to domestication.

In tune with this discussion, Sousa Santos suggests an "epistemology of the

South," with South understood as a metaphor for human suffering caused by capitalism, and with its main objective the reinvention of social emancipation beyond critical theory produced in the North and the social and political praxis that it sponsored. Each culture has a way of organizing these relationships of politics and power. This is reflected in two abysmal dualities: North-South and East-West. It would be naive not to recognize that these two fractures continue to be exposed in the political discussion of the contemporary world.

This epistemology of the South, then, refers to discussions on colonialism and postcolonialism. The postcolonial perspective (which has also, and more appropriately, been called neocolonial) suggests that when one starts out from the margins and the peripheries, the structures of power and knowing become more visible. Out of this comes an interest in the geopolitics of knowledge, which questions who produces knowledge, in what context, and for whom. So it is not enough to "apply" critical theories, to elaborate a possible systematization of knowledge, and also to continue doing what one is and has been doing. It is necessary to question who produces knowledge, when, and to what end.

Not without reason, there is an ever more urgent need for a plurality of collective projects articulated in a nonhierarchical fashion that pay attention to processes of translation, processes that are there to substitute the formulation of an overarching theory with one increasingly more specific and localized. It is not a matter of proposing the end of utopias, but a matter of recognizing plural and critical utopias, or, as Foucault proposed (1966), utopia as a place outside of all places. Foucault dreamed of a science that had as its object different spaces, counterspaces. This science would study not utopias but heterotopias, a kind of heterotopology outside of the paradigms already taken for granted for the most part by what we call modernity.

Central European modernity is the sociocultural paradigm constituted from the sixteenth century onward, and consolidated between the late seventeenth and the mid-eighteenth centuries. This is the period that the West calls modernity.[6] There is, then, a social regulation controlled by three principles: the state, the market, and the community. When Foucault proposed a microphysics of power, he suggested a displacement of both the space of analysis and the level on which it was carried out. The peripheral powers no longer appeared to be necessarily confiscated and absorbed by the state. The market broadened its activities, creating new rules of power allied with rules of employability, and the idea of community was more and more indistinguishable from that of society.

Sousa Santos identifies a malaise in the fractures of cognitive processes that look into who we are, in the spaces and the times that we live in. The world is supposedly globalized, but the rules of living together are not always clear. There is a kind of participation that renders differences performative. It can block the creation of alliances. The colonized subject, Sousa Santos observes, always suffers from a deficit of representation under their own name.

We are living in a time of repetition that allows the present to sweep away the past and the future. There are various names for movements that look to the future as "revolution and progress," but the outcome of the struggle is predetermined. All the difficulties associated with thinking through a social transformation and elucidating it rest upon the collapse of theories of history that got us here in the first place and that have already been called into question by Nietzsche and Heidegger, among others. Many assumptions were eroded. For the defeated, the idea of progress makes no sense, because it was precisely in the context of that historical process that their loss was created. The repetition of the present is unbearable for some and longed for by others. Once again, the key is found in how it is: as the account of something that happened, or as a resource capable of activating the future.

In the past fifty years, many societies have found themselves going through a period of division. A minor change can produce a great number of transformations in unexpected ways. That puts the system in a precarious situation. According to Sousa Santos, more and more questions are being raised as to the nature of roots, especially what roots of identity might be. Nonetheless, controversies arise. After so many discussions about the end of history, posthistory, irreversibility, and the nonsequential nature of time, would it still be sufficient to utilize formulations that legitimize the notion of root and origin?[7]

The twentieth century began with a socialist revolution, and the twenty-first century set in place an introspective revolution that in many cases began with the revolution of the body; due to the fact that the central importance the notions of social class and the psyche had accrued was ultimately assumed by the body, just as Foucault had predicted. Today, Sousa Santos considers the body to be the option of all options, in the same way that the modern age seemed to confirm an overabundance of reason. But the body continued to be translated as object, more specifically as a piece of merchandise, one even suitable for being commercialized and sold for its parts (literally as in the case of organ transplants, or symbolically, as in the porn industry or the sex trade). So this, like so many other "changes," is nothing more than an inversion, suggesting once again the same line of investigation: What good is a critical theory of knowledge if it still appears unable to put changes into effect? And what does it mean to criticize Cartesian thought starting from a moment in which the mind/body dualism is as persistent as ever?[8]

So we have to know what we are talking about and understand that all discourse is a form of action. That is why it is not enough to tell a story about reality or the past. In addition, it is about more than just value judgments or opinions. What we need is to identify past experience in connection with the present and the future, as a resource for generating movement. Bestowing dynamism to the past is recognizing it from the basis of a discontinuous and genealogical form of logic.

The homogeneous repetition of the present would imply an end to permanent interrogations, eliminating all ambiguities and destabilizations. For that reason, Sousa Santos states that without the tension of time it is impossible to think about social transformation; only conformism and passivity would exist. In his view, it is necessary to regain the capacity to be frightened. Every image that can be created as destabilizing is only efficient if widely shared. Destabilizing subjectivity is a poetic subjectivity but also a social construct that is, in turn, an exercise in liminality because it implies experiencing marginal forms of subjectivity. That is because this form of subjectivity of modernity—one based on a subject that imbues it with his or her own particular and invariable essence—no longer makes any sense.

Bhabha (2003) delves deeper into the topic of a commitment to theory, calling our attention to translation once again a political act. He acknowledges that theory has been considered a language of the elite, of the privileged. It is as if there had been a "pure theory," exempt from the demands and the historical tragedies of the majority. This is why Bhabha identifies the binary of theory-political action along with the more common one of theory-practice.

Centuries ago there was a proliferation of serial counterpoints between oppressor and oppressed, center and periphery, negative and positive images, and so on. But somewhere between that metatheorization and the politically engaged radical experience of the "Third World," one can see a specular image of the ahistorical polarity of the nineteenth century that marks the fracture between East and West. In the name of progress and exclusionary imperialist ideologies, modeled on the formulation of "I and the other," oppositional cultural practices proliferate.

I and the Other, Bhabha explains, can be many different things. Those who know and those who don't, those who know in theory, those who know in practice, those who have known longer, those who are beginning to know. What matters is whether some theories considered the new languages of critical theory—such as semiotics, poststructuralist thought, deconstructionist criticism, and so many others—only reflect geopolitical divisions and their spheres of influence, or whether these Western theories do not in fact seem complicit in the hegemonic role of the West as a power bloc.

It would be a sign of political maturity to accept different forms of political writing whose effects would be obscured when distinguishing between theorist and activist. The difference between the pamphlet used by striking workers and the speculative article about theory of ideology, is, according to Bhabha, in their operational characteristics. Both are forms of discourse and produce their objects of reference. Nonetheless, a pamphlet has expository purpose limited to an event, and an article is directed more to the established political principles on which the right to strike is based. They exist side by side. Each cannot see the Other's face. Theories usually stay cloistered inside their passports, but Bhabha prefers the margins of cultural displacement that confuse each and every profound or authentic sense of national culture, once the cultural and historical hybridity of the postcolonial world has been established as paradigmatic point of departure. To do that, he investigates the kinds of tensions and ambivalence that mark this enigmatic place from which theory speaks. What is true or legitimate in this context? Everything seems marked by the ambivalence of meanings that constructs "counterknowledges" in the act of negotiation.

Textuality is not simply a second-rate ideological expression or a verbal symptom of a subject. The problematic of political judgment cannot be represented as an epistemology of appearance and reality, of theory and practice, or of words and things. It also cannot be represented as a dialectical problem or a symptomatic and constitutive contradiction of the materiality of the real. The language of criticism becomes efficient when it does not maintain the separation between master and slave, merchant and Marxist, when it transcends the bases of opposition given and opens space for translation. This is the place of hybridity, where the construction of a new political object (neither one nor the Other) changes the forms of recognition in politics.

The challenge lies in conceptualizing the time of political action and understanding as a means of inventing a spatiality that can accept and regulate a differential structure without producing a unity of opposing forces or being content with adding to the long series of contradictions. Paradoxes and ambivalence send a signal that history is happening inside the systems we construct. It is more a matter of negotiation with the Other than it is a denial.

In this sense, the function of theory in the political process becomes two-fold. On one side, it calls attention to the fact that our points of reference and political priorities do not exist as a primordial form of common sense. They only make sense in historical and philosophical tension and in cross-reference with other objectives. In accordance with Bhabha, there is no community or mass of people whose historicity emits "correct signals." For that reason, the act of negotiation/translation always needs to be interrogatory. The type of question that is formulated is one that is going to show the place of differences, like a disciplinary phantasm or a process of mediation. The Other is normally quoted, mentioned, lit up, boxed in images and counterimages. There is a difference between dealing with the field of cultural difference and dealing with that of diversity. Cultural diversity is an epistemological object, while difference is the process of cultural enunciation, more in line with a previous system of cultural identification.

Sloterdijk explains that, curiously, the most ancient definitions of theory are similar to looking serenely out the window. It could be an exercise of contemplation, whereas in the modern age, when knowledge explicitly came to mean power, it took on the character of work. Windows are those clearings where people are transformed into beings capable of theorizing. For Sloterdijk, a clearing is both a battlefield and place of decision and selection, as Nietzsche made explicit:

> Bescheiden ein kleines Glück umarmen—das nennen sie Ergebung! ... Sie wollen im Grunde einfältiglich Eins am meisten: dass ihnen Niemand weh thue. ... Tugend ist ihnen das, was bescheiden und zahm macht: damit machten sie den Wolf zum Hunde und den Menschen selber zu des Menschen besten Hausthiere. [*Also sprach Zarathustra: Ein Buch für Alle und Keinen* (Chemnitz: Verlag von Ernst Schmeitzner, 1884), 26–27]

> To modestly embrace a tiny bit of happiness—that is what they call resignation. ... At heart they naively want one thing most of all: that no one hurt them. To them, virtue is what makes them modest and tame. With it they turn a wolf into a dog and human beings themselves into people's best house pets. (as quoted in Sloterdijk 1999, 39)

This is the fundamental conflict that the thinker postulates for any and all futures: the struggle between those who create human beings to be small and those who create them to be great. This dilemma, as Sloterdijk affirms, plays out "between the humanists and the superhumanists, the friends of Man and the friends of Superman" (1999, 41).

In Brazil during the first decade of the twenty-first century, these debates have been reformulated in ways that pose rather formidable challenges, as is the case of the hypotheses set forth by Eduardo Viveiros de Castro (2008, 2009). According to this author, the subject/object duality is one of the fundamental questions that many disciplines commit themselves to, particularly anthropology (which is his own field of study). Just as the postulates of psychoanalysis were questioned by Gilles Deleuze and Félix Guattari in *Anti-Oedipus* (1968), Viveiros de Castro presents the Anti-Narcissus, rethinking his own life and profession. This is because traditional anthropologists, like other researchers, place themselves in front of the communities that they study, like a subject in front of an object. It is from this pedestal, as a Narcissus-like subject, that they observe the object to be analyzed. What Viveiros de Castro argues is to abandon the traditional notion of "imagining an experience," opting for "experiencing the imagination." In this sense, production ceases to the main object of analysis. The new key is in becoming.[9]

It is not at all easy to change traditional methodologies. Nevertheless, it seems to be a necessary approach when facing political crises that increasingly reveal the insistent modern schism separating nature and culture, humanity and animality, civilization and barbarism. The Indigenous American perspective studied by Viveiros de Castro points out some new directions, recognizing common conditions, states of being where bodies and names, the self and the Other, penetrate each other, submerged in the same pre-subjective or pre-objective environment (2009, 34).

In absolutely different situations, these gray areas between humanity and animality, nature and culture, have also emerged in the discussion of what is called "bare life" (*vita nuda, zoë*), especially in the way that Agamben would have it. In a way, from the Indigenous American cosmologies to the Nazi concentration camps, resistance seen in the face of such devastation is pronounced on the margins and becomes ever clearer, because being marginal is much more than a location, it is also a way of understanding and feeling life and death in the flesh.

## Exposure to Death, Gray Areas, and the Risk of Becoming Anesthetized

Every living being is exposed to death. As with sex, death has alternated between taboo and fetish over time, appearing in different forms of representation. In the Victorian age, for example, it was quite common to take photographs of the dead to keep as a remembrance, but today it seems in supremely bad taste, especially with the death of children.

The timing of death has also changed. After World War I, the duration of a wake was shortened abruptly due to the sudden increase in the number of deaths. Modern death was sped up and isolated in hospitals or asylums, most of the ceremonies disappeared, and mourning became strange and out of style.

Philippe Ariès (1974) has already shown how in the West, bit by bit, death had become invisible and prohibited, to the point of being considered a taboo. It was only after 1980 that we witnessed a full-scale return to a discussion of death, largely due to the HIV/AIDS epidemic and the movements that arose out of it at that time to draw attention to those dying of the disease.

Jonathan Dollimore (2001) has shown how these fluctuations of visibility and invisibility of death come and go, identifying an ambivalence in the ways that death has been represented. Exposing it to the extreme can also generate invisibility.

In order to analyze the exposure to death today, therefore, it is necessary to enter a space outside of the clichés of death as taboo. Paul Virilio (2002) studied the mass production of cadavers and concluded that, after the Holocaust and so many other mass exterminations, such as those in in Rwanda and Cambodia, it became very difficult to argue that death had become invisible or prohibited, because it was happening all the time and seemed more visible than ever. What has changed is the way that its exposure generates a form of politically organized death, including by way of bureaucratic planning and governmental intervention, as denounced by Zygmunt Bauman (1999). As he sees it, in order to study "modern death," it is first necessary to understand modern power and its ambivalence. One only need observe how normal it is for brutal military interventions to be accompanied by humanitarian aid. Noam Chomsky has often called this phenomenon "the new militarist humanism."

Studies of death, much like studies of culture, usually involve working with the search for representations. And how would it be possible to think of death without representations? To respond to this question, Benjamin Noys (2005) made a comparative analysis of the work of Agamben and Foucault, particularly the moments in which these authors dedicate themselves to understanding the idea of bare life.

The ancient Greeks used two words to define life: *zoë* (bare life) is the pure and simple fact of being alive, common to all living beings, whereas *bios* indicated one's own way of life, the qualified life of an individual or group. Two of the most important Greek thinkers, Plato and Aristotle, were not particularly interested in natural life, only in qualified life, although they were aware of the simple fact of living. Politics, at least in the way it was understood by Aristotle, differentiated human beings from other living beings, because he based his view on the politicization of language (referring to a community of good and evil, just and unjust, and not simply pleasure and pain).

Foucault and Agamben are probably the European authors who dedicated themselves most deeply to studying the ways that these formulations of life persisted (or didn't) in the contemporary world, creating new relationships. Foucault (1976) observed how on the threshold of the Modern Age, natural life began to be included in the mechanisms of state power, and politics was transformed into biopolitics. If, for thousands of years, humans had been considered living animals capable of a political existence, in the Modern Age they were transformed into animals with a politics in which their life as living beings is questioned. That carried with it a perverse ambiguity: the possibility of protecting life through political strategies and, at the same time, the authorization for its extermination. Thus, on one hand, biopower gave qualification to the lives of living beings, while, on the other, it produced the docile bodies it needed. Foucault showed a double political link that relied on political techniques like surveillance (the state takes on the natural act of caring for the lives of individuals) and the study of technologies of the self, strengthened all the more through processes of subjectification.

These were the points of ambivalence that intrigued Agamben. At the beginning of his *Homo Sacer* trilogy, he looked into what the point of intersection between the juridical-institutional model and the biopolitical model of power would be. That is because from this point onward, the author arrived at the original epicenter of the debate, which was the implication of bare life in the political sphere through the act of sovereign power. The production of the biopolitical body is, so to speak, the contribution of sovereign power, but there is a hidden link between power and bare life. When Aristotle differentiated between living (*zen*) and living well (*eu zen*), he was proposing politics as the place in which living must be transformed into living well. So there was a need to politicize this understanding of bare life. But this relationship was not always clear. For Agamben, the issue is one that remains to this day: to comprehend how the space of bare life, originally located on the margins of order, gradually comes to coincide with the space of politics. In his view, exclusion and inclusion, outside and inside, *bios* and *zoë*, de jure and de facto have all entered a gray area, and in order to understand that area better, he considers it fundamental to study the life that can be killed but never sacrificed, that of *homo sacer*, the state of exception and the field as the biopolitical paradigm of the West.

Just as with other authors mentioned earlier, Agamben points out that Western culture became ever more thanato-political, that is, dominated by the politics of death, increasingly exposing all of us to death and power. That process stripped death of its meaning to a certain extent, as Josef Stalin had already made evident when he stated that a single death was a tragedy, but millions of deaths were nothing but a statistic.

The figure of Roman law, *homo sacer*, is exemplary in this sense because the *homo sacer* could be excluded without any penalty from society; and because this agreement appears in the text of the legal code, it is included in the statute of power only in order to be excluded. The enigma of the term *homo sacer* is in the fact that this man was sacred but could not be sacrificed. As far as one can tell, the name comes from a time in which religious law and penal law were one and the same; thus, being condemned to death was also a sacrifice to the divine, although the *homo sacer* did not himself have the right to sacrifice. One possible reason for this, Agamben says, is that what is sacred, *sacer*, already belongs the gods; it is not necessary to become their property through a new act of sacrifice. He could thus be eliminated with impunity and without any sacrificial ritual in order to be converted into an object of the gods. The *homo sacer* was thus situated at the crossroads between those who could be killed and those who could not be sacrificed: that is, outside of human law (there is no punishment for his death) and outside of divine law (there is no need to sacrifice him to convert him into property of the gods). *Homo sacer* was part of an original political structure situated in an area that preceded the distinction between sacred and secular, religious and juridical.

This situation is also related to another condition of the outer limits, which is precisely that of sovereignty. That is because the sovereign power is simultaneously inside and outside of the juridical ordinance. They have the power to suspend any and all ordinances, and for that reason must be outside of the law. At the same time, in order to have this guaranteed power, they must be part of it. The paradox of their existence is in the recognition of the law outside of itself.

The exception that defines sovereignty is thus very complex and challenges the usual dichotomies of inside and outside, private and public, what is one's own and what is someone else's. Contrary to what we tend to think, exception is not what is set apart from the rule, but the rule itself suspended to make space for exception. That is because, curiously enough, when suspended, the old rule is constituted as a new one. In other words, the relationship of exception is one that includes something only by way of its exclusion. It is neither a de facto nor a de jure situation.

One of the evolutionary reasons for the emergence of exception is likely related to the statement that there is no existing norm that can be applied to chaos. It is necessary to create an area of indifference between external and internal, chaos and normality, which is called a state of exception. It arises when a particular territory becomes possible for the first time. That is to say, *homo sacer* and the state of exception are the most important precedents for those recurrent situations, then and now, of inclusion solely for exclusion.

Agamben explains that if exception is the structure of sovereignty, that does not make it an exclusively political or juridical concept. In addition, it is not a power outside of the law, nor is it a supreme norm. It is the original structure in which the law relates to life and includes it through its own suspension. In many ways, this indicates that the law's original relationship with life lies not in its application, but its abandonment.

In set theory, this becomes quite clear, particularly because it includes a distinction between belonging and inclusion. A term can belong to a set without being included and can be included in a set without belonging to it. In political terms, Alain Badiou (2001) explains that belonging is linked to presentation and inclusion is linked to representation. Therefore, a term belongs to a situation if it is presented and counted as units in that situation, such as individuals who belong to a society by existing in it. However, a term is only included in a situation if it is represented in the meta-structure, as is the case with the state. We can consider of the example of voting citizens. It is not enough to be present; it is also necessary to have representation, to have a voice.

Agamben explains that during the Middle Ages, the character victimized by inclusion for the sake of exclusion was the bandit (from the Italian *bandito*, from the verb "to banish"). His situation was that of someone banished from society by sovereign power and exposed to death by just cause. German and French had the term of half-man, half-wolf (*Werwolf* or *loup garou*), the bandit who had lost his political and social rights and had come to be considered sub-human, and for that reason completely exposed to bare life.

The so-called state of exception, conceptualized as an area in which there is no clear distinction between belonging and inclusion, inside and outside, is always a herd-like relationship, a band of the banished. This does not only mean being placed outside of the law or being indifferent to it, but also abandoned, put at risk. Often, one cannot determine whether the banished fall outside or within the realm of ordinance.

The life of the bandit represents the limit of indifference and of passage between other animals and humans, exclusion and inclusion, like a werewolf who paradoxically lives in two worlds without living in either. In many cities, the structure of the band or pack reproduces and proliferates. It is in cities, above all in large metropolises, that banishment from sacred life is possible. The countryside is the space that opens up when the state of exception begins to become the rule.

This countryside or "campsite" (understood as a concentration or extermi-nation camp) became a recurrent theme in Agamben's work and has clear con-notations. The presence of bare life weakens the line of distinction between life and death, between being exposed to death or not. It inevitably established a gray area (or a zone of indistinction).

This expression was proposed by Primo Levi when analyzing the role of some prisoners of Auschwitz who, despite being Jewish, were in the service of the Nazis. In some situations, the channel connecting victim and executioner was lost: the oppressed became the oppressor, and the executioner appeared to be a victim. According to Levi, it had to do with a gray area that represented the alchemy between good and evil, an area where traditional ethics reached a melting point. This area, which is configured as one of irresponsibility or *impo-tentia judicandi* (Levi 1989, 60), is not beyond good and evil, but before it. This *before* seems more important than the *after*, once it exposes the subhuman con-dition on the other side of the posthuman. This also refers to what Hannah Arendt (1992, 252) called "the banality of evil."

Who can make with absolute certainty the distinction between victims and enemies? This gray area can be identified, even today, in many other situations.

Democratic regimes, for example, were established to put an end to sovereign regimes but in fact did not extinguish sovereign power, which still manifests itself in a number of different ways. For example, in 1679, habeas corpus was established, which ensured physical presence in a court of law and became a way of exhibiting the body. More recently, in the search for terrorists, many people have been arrested without any rights. Once again, the body becomes exposed. New methods of political tattooing have arisen, such as the need to be fingerprinted before entering certain countries, businesses, and banks—a trend that appears to be increasingly widespread.

In this situation, Jean Baudrillard (1993) concludes that despite all the attempts to banish the death of culture by a wide range of simulations, it returns and avails itself of the same mechanisms, offering criticisms in unexpected and unusual environments. Not without reason, there is a proliferation of movies about the living dead. In the sequel to the 1968 film *Night of the Living Dead* by George Romero (*Dawn of the Dead*, 1978), zombies invade a mall, one of the main centers of capitalist consumption. This could be a metaphor for how, without knowing or truly understanding it, we quite often behave like these living dead in our own lives.

Alongside media representations, a kind of distribution of vulnerability occurs, one that is no longer limited to mental institutions, terrorist factions, or people who have contracted a virus like HIV/AIDS. Often this vulnerability extends to entire countries, as is the case with Iraq, or continents, such as Africa.

No one doubts the relationship between death and power, but explanations for it vary. Noys observes that Foucault, particularly from the end of the 1970s on, began to see power no longer as sovereign, but as ubiquitous. Agamben agrees to a certain extent, but observes that power is the political power of death, whereas for Foucault death is the limit of power, the moment in which one escapes from it, configured as the most private thing there is in human existence. Agamben goes on to point out that death took on its most virulent form in the case of Nazi extermination camps. It is for this reason that he suggests the countryside (*campo*) as the biopolitical paradigm of the West. His argument is that even with the decentralization of power acknowledged by Foucault there is a certain topology of sovereignty, related to the very understanding of what topology is or might be, as a set of properties that remain unchanging. For Foucault, modern power is power over life, biopolitics or biopower. If sovereign power exposed us to death, modern power invests more and more in life, although not infrequently it also lets us die. This investment is a control over all steps of life, regulating the behavior of the body.

Agamben agrees with Foucault in recognizing power as biopower, but he also observes that it has always been that way, not just from the start of the modern age. Moreover, he questions the extinction of sovereign power. For Agamben, sovereign power also seems to have entered an indistinct or gray area. It is no longer localized in the figure of a sovereign power, but rather spread throughout the social body.[10] The space of sovereignty is neither secure nor stable. If bare life at first seemed exposed in states of exception, now it was rendered banal. It is in the administration of death that Agamben identifies the basis of power.

In this context, the rise of concentration camps is nothing more than the result of the fragmentation of sovereign power in the gray areas that have come to characterize modern life. The camps destabilize the permanent and visible localization of power. This results from the inability of modern nations to inscribe bare life within a territory and a political order. These camps are linked not only with World War II but with the proliferation of refugees created by the new geopolitical configuration of the world. The state of emergency or state of exception became the rule. What Nazism and dictatorships in Latin America have shown is the possibility of combining sovereign power and biopower, in addition to the power to make one live or die. More than a death factory, the camps could be considered a factory of bare life exposed to biopolitics. Zygmunt Bauman (1989) identifies this type of experience as an aspect of modern mentality and social organization, and not of racism in and of itself. According to him, it is the lack of limits on the use of power—and not only racial issues, as it may appear at first glance—that authorizes genocides such as Auschwitz and Hiroshima.

One of the most extreme forms of bare life can be identified in the camps by way of the figure of the *Muselmann* (Port. *muçulmano*, Eng. Muslim), a prisoner in the terminal phase, a kind of walking dead (*mortos-vivos*). These prisoners came to exist in nonspaces where all disciplinary barriers had been destroyed. In their case, it was no longer death that was in question, but the making of dead bodies, as on a mass production line.

When one is free, said Jean Améry (1977), it is possible to think about death without thinking of dying. But not in the camp, where the thought of the ways of dying by phenol injection, gas chambers, or beatings makes the thought of death absolutely superfluous. Death and the production of dead bodies were indistinguishable. Auschwitz was the refutation of every principle of communication. To give a sense of that, the rubber baton that was used to beat the deportees was called "the interpreter" (Ger. *der Dolmetscher*). It ensured the translation of humans into nonhumans, of language into silence, of presences into absences. The translation promoted by "the interpreter" resulted in the impossibility of seeing, knowing, and communicating; *der Dolmetscher* translated human life into bare life.

In the contemporary world, these states emerge from distinct but similar situations, as for example in the cases of the neurological death of people in a coma. The miracle of medicine has created a death that never ends. The limits of life are rethought, as well as the criteria for identifying death. If the decision of the time of death has become an identifier of bare life, then this decision is political and not at all natural. The issue of the coma, for example, is not outside the context of biopolitics; it carries the body once again into a gray area, neither dead nor alive.

For centuries it has been believed that the body signifies when it organizes language (verbal and nonverbal). Agamben, inspired by Emmanuel Levinas (1969), says that language is the appropriation that transforms nature into a face, and this is an important reference for the formation of community. But every human face, even the most beautiful and noble, is inevitably suspended on the edge of an abyss. In order to stay identifiable, it is necessary to maintain communicability. The gesture is the way to make meaning visible; that is why every era that loses its gestures ends up being rendered obsolete by them. The question is how to translate them. How to "read the other" in the face of an absolute lack of distinction between fact and law, and starting from the moment in which all private life has a political and public character (reality shows and platforms like Twitter can be identified as modes of translation of this phenomenon). According to Agamben, it is not that bare life becomes *bios*, thereby producing biopolitics, but that *bios* is continually and increasingly invaded by bare life, to the point in some instances of being only bare life. This has opened up a new field of research and intersections between politics and philosophy, medicine and jurisprudence. Spaces are expanded for legal forms that cannot have a legal form, as is the case for all states of exception. The key words are: indeterminacy, inability to decide, lack of distinction, and, perhaps even more frequently, indifference.

## Excess, Apparatuses, and Malice

In discussing the transgression of anthropomorphism—not only the loss of the human face, as Levinas said, but of the human figure itself—Eliane Robert Moraes (2002, 149) reinvokes Georges Bataille's description of humans as "the only animal that kills its own with fury and obstinacy, yet also the only animal that is disturbed over the death of its own in an absolutely heartbreaking way."

That passage in "Dossier de Lascaux" (Bataille 1979, 322) reappears in various texts of Bataille's, such as in his reflection on the possibilities of human life in the wake of the nuclear catastrophe at Hiroshima in 1945, "À propos de récits d'habitants d'Hiroshima" (1988a, 176–85); or in "La part maudite" (1988b, 61), in which the theme is slavery: "If the slave is undeniably a thing for their master, no one can make a thing of the slave's other self without, at the same time, departing from their inner self, without bestowing on themself the limits of a thing."

The issue of excess and waste, too, is always present. Joseph Roach (1996, 41) makes it clear that in Bataille, violence is always a performance of waste. It is never meaningless, but always has a meaning, absurd as that may seem, because it always serves in some way to create an argument. That is to say, violence is always an excess because in order to create its argument it must expend things such as material objects, blood, environments. These are actions that Bataille identifies as unproductive expenses. Furthermore, violence is always performative and demands spectators, even if it is its own victim or god.

The presence of a god or other kinds of religious apparatuses often reappears in the discussion of power and violence. Slavoj Žižek (1999) raised the idea that the basic tension of the contemporary world is no longer in the reason/feeling dichotomy, as in the eighteenth century, but rather in the tension between knowledge and embodied belief. It has to do not with a specific religion or the recognition of the existence of a god, but with a weakening of the ability to believe in something.

Sloterdijk addressed this same theme in 1983, calling it cynical reason. There was naturally inspiration from Marx and his tracing of the contours of ideological ignorance, the claim that "they do not know it, but they do it." However, Sloterdijk interprets this phrase as "I know what I'm doing, but I still do it," and Žižek completes it: "this is because I no longer know what I believe in" (Žižek 2003, 5).

This doing for the sake of doing without any sort of belief is always guided by what are known as apparatuses of power. Foucault has extensively explored this theme in his work, but it is Agamben (2008) who makes the violence-power-religion relationship even more explicit, recalling a kind of theological genealogy of economics concerning the first centuries of the Church (from the second to the sixth centuries).

The Greek term *oikonomia* meant the management of *oikos* (the home). It was not a theory, but a praxis, as Aristotle explained. Priests introduced this term in theology, deflagrating the trinity of divine figures: the father, the son, and the Holy Spirit. God, as being and substance, would be one, but *oikonomia* (the way one manages home, life, and the world), would be threefold. Christ would take care of the economy, administration, and government of human history.[11]

Theologists, Agamben explains, often distinguished between a theological discourse and a *logos* of economics. It was through *oikonomia* that the dogma of the Holy Trinity and the idea of a divine providential government of the world were introduced into the Christian faith. Action (both economic and political) has no foundation in its being, making it a kind of heritage with no rhyme or reason that theological doctrine has left to Western culture, which Žižek identifies as lack of belief.

The relationship between apparatuses of power and violence was studied particularly by Foucault, at first as positivity, when he was studying with Jean Hyppolite, who borrowed the term from Hegel when referring to the historical element, its rules, its rites, and the institutions imposed on individuals by an external power internalized in belief systems. But Foucault wanted to investigate the concrete ways in which apparatuses behave in games of power, thus giving new dimension to the discussion. Agamben expanded the debate even more, defining apparatus (2008, 40) as anything that has the ability to capture, direct, determine, intercept, model, control, or secure the gestures, conduct, opinions, and discourses of living beings.

Religion, in his view, has a key role in taking things, places, animals, or people from common use to a separate sphere. Every separation therefore would present a religious core and a dose of sacrificial violence. It is sacrifice that regulates the separation, as Marcel Mauss explained in 1899. The rituals vary from culture to culture, but the mechanism of separation is always present. According to Agamben, the counterapparatus that deals with this most efficiently is desecration, because to desecrate is to remove from the sphere of the sacred or to restore to common use what the sacrifice had separated.

The problem today, Agamben explains, is that every apparatus involves a process of subjectivation without which it would function not as a governing apparatus, but only as an exercise of violence. In capitalism's current phase, apparatuses act less as producers of subjects and more as triggers of desubjectivation. The creation of docile bodies that Foucault identified becomes increasingly transformed into the construction of inert bodies. These are citizens that execute everything they order, allowing themselves to be controlled in all instances—from everyday gestures to health, entertainment, and nutrition.

It is this inertia that also makes viable what Adi Ophir calls the language of evil. His treatise *The Order of Evils* (2005), whose subtitle is "toward an anthology of morals" (in the plural), seeks to identify the language of evil or a kind of idiom that has allowed people to express evil as part of reality, a daily routine, designating it not as a diabolical element that transcends reality, nor as an unreal and insignificant lack of good, but as part of what it is. Therefore, it's not about confronting "the sources of evil" in a human essence (in the body or the soul) or in a determined political regime. Ophir's treatise examines the historical, social, and unnecessary production of evil as everything that makes people live precariously with pain, suffering, loss, humiliation, damages of all kinds, terror, alienation, and profound sadness.

People harm one another, intentionally or not, consciously or not, in a group or as individuals. Ophir identifies suffering and loss as the two fundamental types of evil. In these situations, moral discourse finds new limits, and sometimes turns into an immoral attitude by sheer relative indifference to what one could call superficial evils.

Indifference is not a given mental or genetic trait. It is much more a way of relating that threatens sensitivity, manifesting itself as a blindness structured by a limited field of vision, discourse, and action. The proposal is to dislocate the discussion both in the field of theology, which references the impossibility of Evil (Satan or otherwise) in a world created by a benevolent God, and in psychology, which continues to discuss whether humans are born evil, whether evil resides in humans, and so on. In order to discuss everyday evil and its indifference, Ophir instead considers it most useful to observe experiences in light of sociology, economics, political science, geography, and ecology. As such, traces of transcendence that characterize some discussions on morality in the field of philosophy must also be set aside in order to hold human beings accountable for what they do or fail to do in the various forms of coexistence, without any possibility of escaping to a heaven or hell.

There will always be a discourse, a point of view, and a type of preoccupation for the organization of morality. These three aspects, according to Ophir, frame a situation and pave the path to excess. Evil never appears to be what it is. There are evils, in the plural, with important objectives and subjective aspects. Ethics, systems of morality, and normative codes are not seen as Evil, but rather designate (refer, show, trigger, recall, commemorate, predict, and prevent) and interpret a series of incidents of suffering, pain, loss, harm, and ruins that should never happen.

More than discussing moral judgment, Ophir focuses on concrete moral questions relative to things, superfluous evils, intentionalities, interests, and in attempts to disrupt the order of production and distribution of these evils. His work is an anthology of morals in that it discusses morals in the plural as part of what exists and not as an abstract entity or anything of a generalizable nature. There is no reduction to relations of production, desire for power, libidinal aptitudes, or any other kind of a priori data that "determines" the production of evil. Present situations and specific modes of organization are what matter.

Of course, this does not imply a negligence of the past. Part of the systemic comprehension of the situation is not to be indifferent to the fact that we live in a world haunted by testimonies of Auschwitz and Hiroshima, by terrorisms of every kind, by new nuclear threats, by ecological catastrophes, by the actions of the globalized capitalist market, by new networks of information, and by the immediate availability of any and every thought or action. In a way, Ophir's proposal is also inspired by Foucault's ontology of the present, in the sense that it investigates what is ultimately happening and what the historical and epistemological conditions for philosophically examining the historical present are. It is thus no longer possible to separately discuss issues that relate to ourselves, to a particular point in time, and to the forms of evil that appear there.

Hiroshima and Auschwitz, evoked as some of the supreme symbols of evil, are first and foremost events from which human destruction started to become a real possibility. It is not by chance that they are still present in so many academic conferences and diplomatic congresses, in news and memories of all who were involved.

Ophir's work is as fragmented as his object of study. He exposes, step by step, phenological description, as well as its incomplete nature. These descriptions are cumulative and jump around without creating a final dialectic or systemization. Some of the points addressed are disappearance as a category of experience; loss, damage, and presence (also considered a category of experience); excitement and suffering.

Evil, for Ophir, would therefore be a set of evils and their organization. Evil is localized. It is not an abstract entity. It is not given a priori. It necessarily implies a territorialization.

## 2

# Metaphoric Epidemics

## *The Appetite for Deterritorialization*

The act of territorialization has been defined by philosophers and ethologists as the possibility of qualifying an environment, displacing it from one context to another (and therefore creating new ones). It involves a concomitant act of deterritorialization, one in which there is always displacement. It is not about an exclusive relationship with space (a change in location), but rather a signic reorganization that creates new metaphors and mediations. In order not to create conceptual confusion it is important to remember, in accordance with George Lakoff and Mark Johnson (1980), that metaphors are not just figures of language or a product of poetic imagination. They speak to every kind of displacement of thought and action. The authors consider our conceptual system itself, in terms of what we think and how we act, to be of a fundamentally metaphoric nature. Metaphors are, in this way, the point of departure for all cognitive processes and, for that reason, are of utmost importance for processes of territorialization and deterritorialization.

The notion of anthropophagy, so dear to discussions of Brazilian culture, can also be considered a metaphoric strategy and one of territorialization, as it involves simultaneous acts of recognition of otherness, embodiment, and exposition. It tests radical acts of translation beyond the poetic presuppositions of the Brazilian Modernists,[1] especially when it leads us back to the practice of the indigenous Tupinambá. This practice had to do with a complex ritual of death and of devouring enemies of war. As has been explained by anthropological specialists, this ritual could last for years, and what is known as "cannibalism" represented only one of its stages. Eduardo Viveiros de Castro explains that "after having killed the enemy, the executioner changed his name and was marked by scarifications on his body during a prolonged and rigorous period of seclusion" (Castro and Cunha 1986, 59). In this way, a prisoner could live for a long time in captivity before finally being killed in the public square. Decorated with feathers and paint, the prisoner battled his killer in "dialogues of arrogance" until finally being struck dead with the *Ibirapema* (wooden club), which shattered his skull so his body could then be devoured through a ritual of distributing its parts.

Regardless of how cruel this may seem, other than the ritual of cannibalism, these practices can be considered the primary metaphors for translation: expose the other to death (or what it was originally), and devour and distribute its parts.

Clearly there are differences between the cascading metaphors that emerge from cannibalism and the actual scene of the ritual, which was longer and more complex. With the passage of time, names accumulated on the body of the killer, accompanied with drawings etched into the flesh. That means that the existence of "the Other" came to form part of the killer. According to the Jesuits, despite these "savage" practices, the Tupinambá were quite receptive and were not resistant to the teachings of the Catholic Europeans. The problem is that, with the same ease with which they learned these teachings, they just as easily forgot or abandoned them. Thus, what for the priest was "the inconstancy of the savage soul," as Viveiros de Castro himself (2008) has already made clear, in fact revealed the lack of one's own feeling or individual essence: the detachment and the freedom to unmake oneself from elements of one's own culture, to absorb elements of newness, and also to have the freedom to set those elements aside when they lost their meaning. Anthropophagy was the only aspect of their culture that the Tupinambá never abandoned as it was not confused with cannibalism. The reason for that is that while they were willing to given up this cannibalistic period, they retained the technique of re-membering one's enemy, the other who guaranteed "openness to the unfamiliar, elsewhere, and beyond."

Since that time, anthropophagy has been a strategy (or a metaphor, like all cognitive acts) with an aptitude for territorializing the body. The Brazilian Modernists had already extrapolated the indigenous ceremony, removing the impurities from an ethical formula that occupied a central place in the culture of those peoples as it migrated into Brazilian culture as a whole. This formula, as Suely Rolnik explains, "consisted of recognizing an irreconcilable otherness in ourselves as it is inscribed in the memory of bodies."[2] Its effect was a politics of production both of the self and of the world marked by a continual process of territorialization, resulting from the composition of the others who had been devoured and their marks on the body.

In order to better understand this inevitability of translating/devouring the other in one's own body, I offer three related actions: to represent, to incorporate, and to coevolve.

Despite the persistent debate on the differences between representation and presentation—and their political implications, as Alain Badiou has explained—representation always implies, in some way and to some degree, being there for something or someone, so it depends on the nature of what it refers to. Sometimes representation is a synonym for a referential function of the process (semioticians call this function semiosis, or the intelligent act of signs). But representation can also be the relationship between the mental meaning and the referential object or, in other words, the idea that represents the thing.

Robert Wilson (1999) makes clear how all representation has four fundamental aspects: it is always understood by way of a representation of a message; it is made up of or always represents one or more objects; its relationships are in some way grounded in a body; and these relationships can be interpreted by a human being or by another system of information such as other living beings or different substances. In this way, a liquid can be the interpreting agent of another liquid during a chemical reaction, for example. Wilson also observes how mental representation varies between a computational structure and a state of being. In the history of science there is no consensus regarding the definition of a representation. There are explanations that mark specific periods in the history of the cognitive sciences and that, for the identification of certain pathologies, can be equally useful (Clark 1997). Symbolic representation thus refers to computationalist thought of the 1950s. It allowed for representation only by way of symbols and codes that could then be decoded. In these cases, there was a high rate of predictability, and the content of the communication could be understood like a message. Representation distributed with activation of states already underscored the connectionist aspect of the 1960s and 1970s. In this case, the representation would not necessarily be symbolic. There would be no message to be decoded, since the change of state itself could be considered the "message."

In any case, in its varied instances, representation can be considered as a primary state of communication. It usually represents specific concrete objects, sets, properties, events, states of being in the world, possible or fictional worlds, abstract objects such as universals, numbers, qualities, aspects, or traces of something or someone.

Scientists, philosophers, and semioticians have always been interested not only in the content of these mental representations, but also in the question of where this content comes from, what makes it a representation, and how the connection is made between the respective objects as a kind of insistence of the Real.

There are many ways of describing how content is incorporated. In claiming that all corporeal performance carries and reinvents time and communicational processes, Joseph Roach (1996) is one of the authors who observes the ways that representation can be (and often is) a model or way of being of the thing it represents. This means that the way that we represent the world is the way that external information has the possibility to be internalized within the specific circumstances in which the action unfolds. Cognition is always "situated." In this matter, everything is specific and singular when we consider relationships that are not outside of time. That is to say that cognition is not the representation of an independent world, but a kind of embodied relationship between the world and the mind.

If we go back to Giorgio Agamben's work discussed in the previous chapter, it is clear that in the body it is as if the "state of exception" were in fact the rule, in an eternal gray area between inside and outside, private and public. That is because cognition depends on bodily experience. Our abilities, whatever they may be, are materialized and constituted in biological, psychological, and sociocultural contexts in ways that are inseparable from one another. All visible actions as well as invisible ones are subject to perceptual and sensorimotor processes.

Francisco Varela, Evan Thompson, and Eleanor Rosch (1991) named these cognitive acts *enaction*, that is, the process by which configurations emerge out of the transit between body and environment in the phenomenological, developmental, structural, and evolutionary sense. The body is always a possible and living experiential reality.

Beyond representation, in order to better understand the transit between body and environment, it is helpful to study and pay closer attention to what is called coevolution. This expression derives from the Darwinian term coadaptation or co-option and was utilized for the first time by biologist Peter R. Raven and anthropologist Paul H. Ehrlich in their article "Co-Evolutionary Ethology," published in 1964. In this text, the authors explain the coevolutionary relationship between butterflies and the plants that host their chrysalis, observing how one modifies the other. Some years later, Richard Dawkins (1976) and Charles J. Lumsden and Edward O. Wilson (1979) explained that one needs to be careful so not to confuse things. The cultural behavior patterns are valuable for survival but they are not transmitted genetically, nor are they subject to processes of natural selection as it operates within the scope of genetics.[3] What do exist are analogous situations. Certain cultural norms, for example, survive and reproduce better than concurrent norms, making culture evolve on a parallel path to genetic evolution, only much more quickly. The more agile the rhythm of cultural evolution is, the more fragile the connection is between genes and culture, although the connection is never completely broken. Culture allows for a rapid adjustment to changes in the environment by means of adaptations that are finely tuned, invented, and transmitted with a precise corresponding prescription. In this sense, the better adapted an idea is to its environment, the greater chance of survival it has.

A few of these adaptive strategies radicalized body/environment relationships in such a way that they establish different types of liminal pathologies. They are to some extent an unfolding of the anthropophagic act. In the meantime, what is most characteristic about them is that, in devouring the other, they camouflage, metamorphose, or disarticulate, calling the very notion of themselves into question. At its extremes, it is once again bare life that is presented here, not as somehow separate from biopolitics, but as the operator of its own destabilization.

## *The Pathologies of the Limit: Camouflages, Metamorphoses, and Disarticulations*

The architect Neil Leach (2006) dedicated himself to studying some phenomena that, for the time being, I am considering "pathologies of the limit," and that he calls "identifications" between body and environment. To this end, he proposes a theory of camouflage that begins with identification and other related strategies.

Leach recalls Woody Allen's character in *Zelig* (1983), the eponymous Leonard Zelig, who assimilated to everything around him, like a perfect chameleon. As an architect, Leach was particularly interested in habitable spaces, in what makes a space familiar or foreign, more so than assimilation between people. In this sense, he observes how some prisoners, for example, become so attached to their cells that even once they are freed, they re-create environments that resemble those of their captivity. His model case is Nelson Mandela, who, upon leaving prison, went to live in a bungalow he built himself that looked like a replica of the South African prison. He could have chosen any place to live, but he opted not to abandon the vivid traumas of prison because, confined there, he began to establish an identity very much his own.[4]

The compulsion to return to something familiar characterizes all of us. Home is a set of sounds, smells, visual images, mobilities, and spatial practices. It is fundamentally a set of actions. In the late 1930s, Walter Benjamin (1978) often said that we discover meaning in the world through the discovery of similarities. This idea was developed in his essays "Doctrine of the Similar" and "On the Mimetic Faculty," which inspired Theodor Adorno to discuss the passage of mimesis as a process from passive assimilation to active creativity. Adorno (1968) considered the action of mimesis to be similar to the effects of love, involving a moment of coupling and combination. Leach concludes that assimilation to an environment would inevitably have to do with mimesis.

We must take care in this area. The concept of mimesis varies from author to author. In Leach's work it is characterized by the ability to develop an identification with what is outside, in the external world (different from the internal but not separate from it). Forging a bond between the self and the Other would mean creating an empathetic strategy with the world that seeks an approximation and a creation of similarities. In her doctoral dissertation, researcher Rosa Maria Hercoles proposes another definition of mimesis that I find quite appropriate: an operator that carries the possibility for something to acquire formal existence (2005). The results produced by this process of materialization from possibility into actual existence would remain contingent on the means by which this operator was acting (2005, 27). Mimesis would thus be much more than mere imitation.

In Benjamin, there is even the recognition of mimesis as a creative act in itself. It would be a form of reconciliation between subject and object, processed largely by the imagination, creating a kind of mediation between unconscious and conscious, dreams and reality. It is interesting to observe that, in this case, fantasy is used in the positive sense of the term. It is not something that leads to escaping reality but, on the contrary, is a form of living reality, of instrumentalizing a vision of the world. In the dialectical terms of the Enlightenment, mimesis was constituted by irrationality and could additionally be understood as the "magic of alterity." However, Benjamin will go on to say that the action of mimesis is dependent on a mental state. This would make it important to stay alert to the possibilities of creative imagination. He recognizes with good reason that children have always been most suited to this.

Another author worth mentioning is Roger Caillois (1967). Interested in the phenomenon of mimicry (which is not quite the same as mimesis), Caillois defines it as a modality of play. According to him, there are four types of games, each establishing fundamental relationship categories of the body to the environment, the body to other bodies, and the body to itself.

The first type of game is *agon*, a competition where equal opportunity is artificially created so that the antagonists confront each other in supposedly ideal conditions, therefore giving a precise and indisputable value to the winner's triumph. It has to do with a rivalry that always carries a special quality (speed, continuity, vigor, memory, ingenuity, etc.) and happens within defined limits. This is the game that regulates sporting activities and organizes teams for competition. It is always a competitive game, hence the term "agonistic." In life it can be seen in the game between predator and prey with survival as its final objective.

The second type of game is *alea*, which characterizes and reveals what could be called a game of chance. In this case, the player is passive. They do not demonstrate their qualities and dispositions, or the agility of their muscles or their intelligence. They live in risk: the die is cast (*alea iacta est*). It is a dismissal of desire, an abandonment to one's destiny. Some games, like a match of dominos or cards, combine *agon* and *alea* because, in a way, chance controls the hands of each player. Games of chance seem to be human games par excellence. Animals experience only games of competition, mimicry, and vertigo.

While *agon* and *alea* seem to translate opposite attitudes, they end up obeying the same law: the artificial creation of an ideal situation. This is because, in some way, these games project fictional environments so that the competitions can be established. The difference is in who controls the situation: the players themselves, or the game itself, in a self-organizing action that seems subject to what is known as destiny.

In this attempt to propose a fictitious situation, the third type of game arises, mimicry or the temporary acceptance of an illusion, "in-lusion." In this case, the game is not just about creating an imaginary environment, but about turning oneself into an illusory character. The subject plays with beliefs, believing to be what they are not, or making others believe they are something else. The example Caillois chooses is not from the players, or from art, which would seem to be the most obvious option, but from insects, which are to him the most disturbing examples. This is because some insects do not need to add prostheses, masks, or manufactured accessories. They can change their appearance in order to present hidden morphologies that transform them into their current environment, or configure an inanimate body in the living body. Legendary psychasthenia, for example, is the trance of the eyed hawkmoth (*Smerinthus ocellata*), insects that not only mimic an appearance, but even lose, during crisis, the very notion of space and the ability to create spatialities, causing a return to the inanimate state. Contagion and imitation reach a stage that goes far beyond simulacrum because the fantasy becomes the true state, while being represented in a fictitious state.

Finally, the last type of game studied by Caillois is *ilinx*, the game of vertigo. This game is not restricted to what is understood as vertigo in the ordinary sense, such as the state of dizziness that results from the repetitive and tireless whirling of dervishes. *Ilinx* also includes games of moral vertigo. These always involve some kind of risk. A violent fall, a disappointment, the loss of a loved one, and everything that pushes the body to the limit in some way. Mimicry radicalizes the loss of limits in particular, diluting the notion of self, although all the other types of games proposed by Caillois also involve, in some sense, the destabilization of limits.

Beyond mimicry and mimesis, the other radical strategy related to camouflage, but with specific organizational modes, is metamorphosis. James Elkins (1999) explains that in order to comprehend this strategy, it is necessary to study, before anything else, distortion (Lat. *torquere*, to distort) and deformation (Lat. *deformis*, to deform). These words are related to disproportion, distention, dissolution, dissection, disruption, and disjunction.

In the body, they are characterized by their own processes. Elkins ventures to claim that, in fact, all representation is born in some measure of pain and metamorphosis. To demonstrate this hypothesis, he proposes the skin (membranes, movement, and cut) as the primary category of pain, since both the outer and inner skin always represent a kind of border (where everything ends or where everything begins). Every action of, on, and in the skin is an action that transits the edges.

In order to focus specifically on metamorphosis, Elkins starts from different experiences. First, he refers to the body's presence, which already implies in itself the possibility of transformation. "To be" is "to be in movement." The second strategy of metamorphosis would be the vision that creates analogies between one part of the body and the rest of it. An important example in the plastic arts is Pablo Picasso, who did much more than propose a formal game of corporeal pieces and perspectives; he practiced different ways of understanding the body and its relationship with the environment. In addition, Elkins proposes hybridizations between the bodies of monsters and the bodies of humans, which suggest an unfamiliar and frequently fragmented organization. The monster figure—different from a monstrosity—has always represented a challenge to the parameters of normality. George Canguilhem explains that the monster would be a body, while a monstrosity is the production of discourse, the circulation of images, and the consumption of every type of sign (1991, 171–72). The monster particularly interested Elkins.

But beyond the presence and the analogy there is still the geometric reduction that would represent the body based on diagrams, logical schemata, and maps, tackling the problem of the impossibility of representation and of the inconceivable. When the body metamorphoses into schemata, there is always an instance of ruin and absence. In this sense, representing the body could mean suggesting what has not been shown and explaining what is needed.

Could this be the gap Agamben speaks of when discussing the testimony of the *Muselmänner* of the concentration camps? In this sense, the gap is not just in what the body cannot take, or in what is not said in the act of bearing witness. The gap that deepens the fissure is the gap of wanting-to-say and losing-ability-to-say, of the gesture that ceases to communicate and exposes its own powerlessness.

This state approaches disarticulation as a strategy of the destabilization of limits. According to Slavoj Žižek (2003), the expression "out of joint" has been a philosophical condition and an issue of conscience and history. Every narrative, in a way, wishes to give a response to the enigma of how things become "out of joint" and why this situation is inevitable. It refers to the subject that seems constitutionally out of place, disarticulated.

As Marjorie Garber (1997) reminds us, Ovid, Pinocchio, Freud, and Shakespeare, among others, inspired metaphors to describe situations, characters, and representations beyond axes. The joints articulate and connect. Aristotle (1984) considered the joints to be the "center." He said that "the whole limb, where the joint is situated, can become one or two, tensed or slack, changing potentially or actually, by reason of the joint." The system that articulates the parts as complex structure is normally called syntax, as if it were an aspect of grammar, the way to articulate. There is, in this sense, a dependency on the theories of language or on the notion of the organic form. This bias becomes interesting when we think about language as the domain of articulations. There is a proliferation of metaphors that often do not necessarily depend on verbal language, but present diverse narratives, blurring the boundaries between ani-mate and inanimate body, as is the case in Heinrich von Kleist's classic *Über das Marionettentheater* (On the Marionette Theater, 1810). In its evolving process, the obsession with marionettes was not only explored in the theater to evoke the ideal actor as a marionette, but reconsidered through technological advancement, in its obsession with replicants, robots, and avatars, as heralded by Ridley Scott's pioneering film *Blade Runner* (1982). It passed from the syntax of sentences, to the syntax of skeletons, to the syntax of political and historical thought and their various translations, including in fictitious, but absolutely real, virtual environments.

Thus, the pathologies of limits appear as a crisis of articulations, the state that enables and sustains bare life as the experience of hyperexposure and excess of reality.

## The Insistence of the Real: The Report, the Abject, and the Crude Phenomenon

Not without reason, cinema and photography have been models for the discus-sion of relationships between ficticious environments and the insistence of the real. Joel Black (2001) highlights André Bazin and Siegfried Kracauer as two important thinkers who reflected on the ontology of the photographic image as a possible example "of non-mediation with reality." Bazin said that photography differed from the other arts by having the object printed on the film emulsion without intermediation from the subject. Cinema, in turn, satisfied our appetite for reality by bringing time to the photographic space.

It is clear that this hypothesis has been debated at various points and radi-cally redimensioned in the passage from photography and film to the digital environment. However, it still generates debate.

Peter Wollen and others will translate this "reality" discussed by Bazin in semiotic terms as "indexicality" or the existential link to the object. In a way, this alleged link has slowly undermined itself in the era of digitalization in the face of so many possibilities, which has provoked a "*saudosismo* of reality," a kind of nostalgia that Black identifies when discussing reality's effect, for example, on so-called reality shows.

Indeed, Black says, reality shows, just like real-time broadcasts online, are no more real than any fiction film. However, they demonstrate a certain necessity, and it is this that seems to interest the many researchers who discuss "the return of the real" (Foster 1996).

Both Bazin and Kracauer (1997) studied the photographic nature of film and its ability to reproduce physical reality. The idea of film as art started being practiced in the 1950s with the emergence of independent films. Noel Carroll (1996) explains that a film can never, in fact, be considered a piece of reality. The issue was always its realistic effect on the viewers.

There is, therefore, a return to the debate surrounding representation. Harold Bloom (1994) said that visual tyranny challenged literature and other representational arts, in that they sought a similarity between interior and surface. But today everything that traditionally refers to the subject's interior, to the individual, becomes part of the effects of illusion, especially in experiences of extreme exposure like Orkut, Facebook, and so forth.

The film has been the icon of the culture of the masses and has documented reality in a number of different ways. Some have opted for historical references, like *Forrest Gump* (1994) and *Titanic* (1997); others have re-created prehistorical references, like *Jurassic Park* (1993) and *2001: A Space Odyssey* (1968); still others have clamored for the status of documentary, like *Amistad* (1997) and *Schindler's List* (1993). There are also those that have explored the world of dreams, like *Un Chien Andalou* (An Andalusian Dog, 1929), and a whole series of productions that have gambled on the illusion of reality with the simulation of disasters, accidents, and so forth.

Black suggests that the real effect increasingly practiced in films is what makes things and situations more explicit. They reveal or ignite, so that something exposes itself in a way that had not yet been done. The private lives of people—intimate, political, sexual situations—everything is in view. This occurs in transit with journalism (which deals in celebrity exposure), in art films, and in the porn industry, for which Japanese culture deserves to be highlighted, which originated some of the most radical and unprecedented experiences, such as *hentai*, which are pornographic animations.

The notion that "nothing should seem unreal" means that "nothing should be invisible"—everything must be exposed. This tendency toward hyperexposure has been tested for many decades. In addition to the cited example by Luis Bunuel, *An Andalusian Dog*, there are several examples like Michelangelo Antonioni's *Blow Up* (1966), in which the photographer records a murder in a park and doesn't even realize what happened until the film is developed, not to mention more recent experiments, especially from China and Iran, that present common people interpreting themselves and blurring the boundaries between fiction and nonfiction.

This practice has sometimes been made explicit by the way a movie is filmed. A great example was *The Blair Witch Project* (1999), in which the actors filmed themselves and, along with an incessant "blaring" of information on the internet, created the legend of the Blair Witch. The production was the process itself. This had already been tested in cinema, but not with box office success of this proportion.

Television, which critics Jean Baudrillard (1993) and Paul Virilio (2003) called a principal crisis of reality, also began to be rethought. This is nothing new. Giambattista Vico (1668–1744) insisted that the human reality was always constructed, centuries before electronic games and reality shows.

Films and other media productions do not compete with reality, but they do compete among themselves and with other productions. The borders between reality and fiction are increasingly more blurred, even in supposedly superrealistic productions like *Saving Private Ryan* (1998), among countless others.

Still in the cinematic medium, the conflict over media representation was brought to the forefront by experiments like *The Truman Show* (1998) and *Pleasantville* (1998). Inversely, the supposed exposition of life in media like *Big Brother* and *Survivor* also puts on airs of fiction in that actions are exposed without any decency. It is well understood that this is a representation and a game with the audience, but what matters seems to be, again, the effect of reality.

Another author who has been studying what is called "rites of realism" is Ivone Margulies (2003), for whom the supposedly realist cinema does nothing but affirm that what we see always relates to an existing reality, to something that we know as a certain landscape, a situation, and so on.

In the 1970s, various cultures discussed this insistence on the real, largely through the affirmation of the carnality of the body, through rituals of possession, animal sacrifice, torture, exposition of physical disabilities, and so on. A question that made itself very present was how, on a two-dimensional screen, cinema could present the depth expressed in live theater. Could cinema be a hybrid medium?

An exemplary case is from the Japanese director Kazuo Hara, who has often made documentaries about a performative enunciation, like in *Extreme Private Eros: Love Song 1974* (1974), which describes the life of his ex-wife, Miyuki Takeda, a bisexual feminist. The audience becomes a voyeur. The private is always regulated from the outside, but Hara's documentaries promote a shift from the public sphere—that is, from what resembled a collective consensus—to the private sphere.

The performative power of his work lies in his ability to establish a practical meaning for the body, in the sense not only of what the body is, but of how it can or cannot negotiate spaces and positions in terms of cultural coordinates. The performative would be not only ritual practice, but an influential ritual practice for subjects that are constantly being reformulated. According to Hara, repetition is always reformulation and quotation.

In the context of Japan, from which Hara speaks, the emphasis on the body in cinema emerged in a more incisive way with the new era of Shochiku Films, inaugurated in 1959 with *Ai to kibo no machi* (A City of Love and Hope), directed by Nagisa Oshima, who was twenty-seven years old at the time, constituting an exception in the cinematic world from the very outset. In 1956, the *Shichinin no kai* (Group of Seven) emerged, proposing a new concept in cinema that reflected on its relationship with reality, specifically with the body, death, and sex. The principal representatives of this generation were, in addition to Nagisa Oshima, Shohei Imamura, Yoshishige Yoshida, Susumu Hani, Hiroshi Teshigahara, Masahiro Shinoda, and Seijun Suzuki, and the documentarian Kazuo Hara himself.

More than the notion of the metamorphosis of the body, present in the monstrous experiences that marked the postwar era, what characterized the experiences of the new directors was the act of exposing the body, challenging key questions like representation, the relationship between life and death, sex as purgation, and so forth.

The basis of realism that they proposed, Lucia Nagib (2006, 131) explains, was "agnosticism, the absence of the metaphysical and of the punitive god of all monotheistic religions."

They also questioned the divine origin of the emperor and his sovereign body. In the new proposals, there was no place for any type of hierarchy. Based on this idea, a kind of radical contamination between subject and object became increasingly more present. The director was not simply an observer or instructor of the scene and the film. Conventional detachment and the notion of the observer are gone for good. And this was considered one of the directions explored after the war, in the sense of searching for an ever-greater closeness and identification with the "bare facts," minimizing mediations and representations (stand-ins) as much as possible.

Often coming from experiences of sex and violence, the artists come to represent more than a simple aesthetic irreverence. There was a political position of resistance to the renewal of the US-Japan Security Treaty. This resistance was supported by the left and the neoformative movement Zengakuren (National Federation of Students' Self-Government Associations), and it was mostly young directors belonging to the Group of Seven—the *nuberu bagu* movement (*nouvelle vague*, as in 1960s France) or the new wave—that proposed the actions. Besides them, there was also the group *taiyozoku* (Sun Tribe), which filmed stories in the street with heavy improvisation and amateur actors who were, for the most part, ordinary citizens and not professionals. One of these examples, analyzed by François Truffaut, was *Kurutta kajitsu* (Crazed Fruit, 1956), directed by Ko Nakahira.

The body, for these artists, was the real ballast, the weight that kept the film afloat. Various boundaries were blurred in succession, between image-object and subject, public life and private life, creating new gray areas. The new cinema should be, above all, personal (of the author) and subjective-active (*shutai-teki*). Paradoxically, it should also wage an incessant negotiation of itself. This meant, once more, that there would be quite a peculiar relationship between the filmmaker subject (*shutai*) and the filmed object (*taisho*), one penetrating the other in an act of breaking boundaries.

Nagisa Oshima's *Ai no korida* (In the Realm of the Senses, or Bullfight of Love, 1976) is another fundamental example. It was commissioned as a pornographic film and explored the story of Abe Sada and Kichizo Ishida in an explicit dialogue with Georges Bataille's *Story of the Eye*. Both in Oshima and Bataille, the transgression begins with the domination of the woman. Simone and Sada want to satisfy their erotic whims, even if the experience ends in death, being taken to the ultimate consequence. Another similarity is the metaphor of the eye. Oshima translated Bataille's voyeuristic eye in *In the Realm of the Senses*. It is what observes the sexual act, but it also is itself the object of penetration and laceration. Bataille's bullfight ends with the bull having its organs eviscerated, but in Oshima it is the character of Kichizo who ends up killed from the amputation of his male sex organ.[5]

All of these metaphors proposed by artistic experiences and cultural rituals refer, in a way, to a return of the real. Foster (1996) interprets this phenomenon as the aspiration to a critical consciousness of both artistic conventions and historical conditions.

Radical, originating from *radix*, refers to the root. But it is not a matter of seeking the recovery or replication of a root or origin; it is about the identification of latent connections. It seeks to connect with an old (sometimes lost) practice in order to disconnect from a present way of seeing/feeling. Foster makes clear that the artists of the 1950s in some ways recycled the ambitions of the avant-garde, and those of the 1960s critically elaborated on them, which in certain countries occurred in the following decades. There is a coarticulation between artistic and political forms.

Thus, if the *readymades* and collages defied the bourgeois principles of artistic expression and "works of organic art," the neo-readymades and neo-collages reinstated these principles and reintegrated them through repetition. If Dada attacked the audience and the market, neo-Dada adapted to them. In protopop, the nouveau-realist reception rediscussed the notion of art-commodity. Marcel Duchamp's urinal can be transformed into Ballantine's bottles and so on.

However, these experiences are all very ambiguous, creating temporal interchanges between the neo-avant-garde and history, a complex relationship of anticipation and reconstruction. The phenomenon cannot be simplified to a logic of cause and effect. What is in question in these transitions is the institutionalization of art that occurs repeatedly in various instances, although the action of resistance seems to be the nature of art.

Freudian psychoanalysis and later studies by Jacques Lacan discussed how an event is only registered on another that recodes it, which means we only come to be who we are through deferential actions. Foster creates an analogy with the artistic phenomena that are always returning but, curiously, to the future and not the past.

The notion of return itself seems fundamental to both postmodernism and poststructuralism. What Foster asks is what this return actually means. The notions of difference, repetition, narrative, causality, temporality, and textuality are pertinent to the discussion. All the authors who approached the theme avoided simplistic common-sense approaches that wagered on the real as synonym of what is, without any mediation.

When it is said that some post-avant-garde analyses tend more toward epistemology than toward ontology, this means that they focus more on the conditions of perception than on formal essences or existential categories from which a definition would be possible.

Once more, there are gray areas. Lacan spoke of *tuché*, Barthes of *punctum*, which would be precisely a kind of area of contamination between inside and outside, subject and world, public and private.

A great example is the artist Cindy Sherman, who constantly evoked the subject under gaze or the subject as framing throughout her film work of 1975–82. There would no longer be a phenomenological immanence, namely, the notion of "I see myself seeing myself," but rather a psychological estrangement, "I am not what I imagined." Sherman seeks precisely to capture the fissure between the true or real images of the body and the imagined.

Her work, like that of other artists, leads to a new discussion regarding the so-called abject, a category of not-being discussed by Julia Kristeva (1982) and before her by Bataille (1922–40) and Louis-Ferdinand Céline (1934). Foster inquires as to whether the abject condition can be transformed into an abject operation and, consequently, into an approximation of the real.

Some texts written in the mid-1930s appear in Bataille's complete works (vol. 2) under the name of "L'Abjection et les formes misérables" (Abjection and Miserable Forms). These were not immediately published, but they became fundamental and are still cited today, since they identified social abjection as a violent force that operates within and beyond the modern state. As has previously been mentioned by Joseph Roach, it has to do with a force that robs masses of their dignity and reproduces them incessantly like a social expense, a hindrance.

To deal with abjection is to recognize the heterogeneity that Bataille studied when identifying another form that the system cannot assimilate and rejects as excrement. At the time, Bataille was developing the idea of attraction and repulsion. The centripetal force of attraction in a society would be the power not of attraction, but of repulsion, having as its sacred core the function of those things classified as abject. This project, which related the sacred to the power of impurity, will be addressed fifty years later by Julia Kristeva when she formulates a theory of abjection.

Kristeva (1982) studies abjection in the context of intertextuality, which was a kind of methodology she had been developing based on the idea that every text always consists of several texts. Unlike Bataille, Kristeva saw the abject not as primarily social, but as philosophical and psychoanalytical. Kristeva is interested in how a connection between subject and object is conceived, since the subject is the psyche, and the object is the whole. The subject is the being that has the capability to act consciously, and the object is the world, what's around. This has been discussed by many thinkers, such as Freud and Lacan. In terms of poetic language, the issue is also addressed by Antonin Artaud, whose writings and drawings encouraged other thinkers such as Jacques Derrida, Michel Foucault, Gilles Deleuze, and Jean-Luc Nancy. The abject would be an intermediary position, neither subject nor object, or what psychiatrists call borderline. It would be a way to explain the condition in which a child is not yet separated from the mother's body and can only do so convulsively, searching for the exit inside itself, as self-abject. This abject, as Kristeva studied it, concerns insurmountable boundaries, indifferential substances.

In fact, we often experience this situation of not recognizing ourselves as object or subject, which is just one more way of proving our incomplete, unfinished, processual nature. The ontological condition of the abject threatens its autonomy and self-definition. This is because, once named, it would cease to exist in its processual character and become recognizable. In bodily terms, the abject would be blood, excrement, mucus, various forms of injury, all of the body's scatology.

In history, as in nature, Karl Marx said when commenting on the work of Bataille, "the loss of health is life's laboratory." It is about an operation of change, in which there are no essential or fixed terms, but only energies in a force field. The energies operate from words that designate the poles of the field, in which they become incapable of holding immediate oppositions.

Bataille was interested in the loss of systems of meaning, in the things that were no longer assimilated in science, philosophy, or the social (such as operations of the state). He sought to explore the meaning of the procedure he will call theoretical heterology. Heterology is connected to every terminal process. The product is always excrement, so heterology is adjacent to scatology. The lowest parts of cities are typically untouchable, much like the parts of the body. The *Lumpenproletariat* is the abject of all social classes and is considered another example of how bare life invades biopolitics. Like the *homo sacer*, the lumpen is qualified, or supposedly included and biopoliticized, only to be banished.

Bataille researched the political alongside the psychosexual, demonstrating the scandal of the identification between the two untouchable heterological elements. Abjection could be both substance (excrement) and theme (gender/genre and degradation) or functional factor. In Kristeva, as we saw, the focus is more around the issue of subject/object. The abject is always the other. It lives in the place where meaning collapses, and therefore there is no desire to designate meaning as there is with objects. The abject is a convulsion, a cry. It lives at the limit of nonexistence and the hallucination of a reality that can annihilate or save, just like solutions from the organism that protect and purge, like spasms and vomit.

Thus, the abject never ceases to examine its territory because it has difficulty dealing with the solid quality. It always appears fluid, unfinished. It is never alert enough to know itself. It must constantly be reminded. Pleasure is what causes the abject to exist as such. Above all, abjection is ambiguity. It does not divide the subject from what threatens it. Instead, it lives in perpetual danger. It is a composite of judgment and affect, of condemnation and desire. Abjection preserves what existed in the immemorial violence by which the body became separate from another body, in order to maintain the obscurity in which the meaning of things perishes and the unimaginable affect is carried. The self becomes heterogeneous and mimics the other. The abject permeates the subject, which becomes the abject. Death is the situation that most violently represents the strange state in which the non-subject has lost its non-objects and is incapable of imagining anything through the order of abjection. Artaud is the inescapable witness of this situation. For him, writing was like resuscitating, dealing with death without mediations given a priori.

The production of the monster and the heterogeneous, through the process that excludes what cannot be generalized, generates an illogical difference, outside of categories constructed to work logically with differences. In this case, we are interested in the invisible instances of connection in which instability seems absolute but sustains itself to the extent that it becomes embodied. Dehumanization, not death, is what matters the most here. The legacy of the *Muselmänner* in Auschwitz, the people starving in Ethiopia, the crack-addicted children abandoned in the streets of São Paulo.

## PART II

# Operators of Resistance

Theories have four stages of acceptance: (1) this is worthless nonsense;
(2) this is an interesting, but perverse, point of view; (3) this is true, but
quite unimportant; (4) I always said so.

(Gerald Edelman quoting J. B. S. Haldane)

We are not equipped to remember or represent anything with fidelity
that we see or perceive in the world. We remember better what seems
relevant to our survival and not all the details involved in different
events.

(Michael S. Gazzaniga)

# 3

# Principles of Experience

## The Profaning Aptitudes of the Organism

### Perception as Cognitive Action

The philosophical formulations that provide the basis for and describe so-called lived experience were European phenomenology (above all those departing from the formulations of Edmund Husserl, Maurice Merleau-Ponty, and Martin Heidegger) and American pragmatism. Since 1950, but particularly starting in the 1980s, the cognitive sciences have given new dimension to the debate, proposing bridges with psychology, neuroscience, linguistics, and cognitive anthropology. Moreover, ecological philosophy, as it became ever more fundamental to this debate, focuses on the relationship between organism and environment, establishing a clear interlocution between ethology and biosemiotics.

As was mentioned earlier, one of the marks of poststructuralism, postmodernism, and postcolonialism was the critique of the concept of the Cartesian subject. In all of these fields of study, some presuppositions were shared such as the rejection of logocentrism and Enlightenment reason, which became a recurrent theme not only among cultural scholars, but also among scientists, most notably those who formulated studies of the embodied mind. At the same time, research showed an increase in complexity. The task of relating different levels of description (within and outside of the organism), the undisciplined nature of the body, and its modes of organization in relation to the environment (Greiner 2005) became all the more evident. In a rather basic (and profound) way, this is what the "reading of the other" is all about.

A fundamental starting point for understanding these transitions between body and environment is the study of perception, which is nothing more than the principle of any and every experience. Contrary to what seemed like consensus according to common sense, perception isn't just an interpretation of sensory messages, but an internal simulation of action, as well as an anticipation of the consequences of that action (Berthoz 2001).

According to Alain Berthoz, one of the first attempts to test this hypothesis was carried out in 1852 by Hermann Lotze, who proposed the spatial organization of visual sensations as the result of their integration with muscular sense. The idea that the pieces of information that determine motor command are used by the brain to "know the movement" was proposed by Hermann von Helmholtz (1962), for whom motor control was capable of comparing sensations with predictions based on motor command.

In 1890, William James also described a neuronal circuit, which anticipated the sensory consequences of movement. For perceptive acts there would be a point of departure determined by a complex object (the prey, for example), but the internally organized representation by the organism would not be restricted to this circumstantial relationship. This means that the perceptive act could also foresee what had not yet occurred. In this way, after the initial simulation, there would be a kind of adaptation to future stimulations subject to being characterized by perceptive leads. So it was necessary to suppress the dissociation between perception and action. Based on these studies, Berthoz proposed the understanding of perception as a simulated action and movement as our sixth sense.

This hypothesis had already been evidenced, according to Berthoz himself, in studies by Pierre Janet (1935), who observed, for example, perception before a chair, even before the act of sitting down. Just observing it, one was already internally simulating the act of sitting down. This imaginative-perceptive phenomenon has also been detected by Merleau-Ponty, who recognized vision as a "touch by sight."

Among scientists, philosophers, and art historians there is a consensus that the phenomenological method of research is an important strategy for recognizing the role of the body in relation to the other and as the foundation of experience. At the same time, it is necessary to note that even within phenomenology there are different components, such as the transcendental idealism of Husserl, the ontology of being-in-the-world of Heidegger, and the mundane phenomenology of Merleau-Ponty, among others. Both Heidegger and

Merleau-Ponty did a critical rereading of Husserl's work, transposing its transcendental idealism into factual existence. The phenomenology of Merleau-Ponty was already heading in the direction of science, because it sought to avoid any kind of idealist return, denying the existence of an "interior man," and recognizing in perception a field of experience that was not configured exclusively as an act of the psyche but was eminently corporeal. So the notion of experience was sufficiently distinct between Husserl and Merleau-Ponty. Husserl understood "phenomenon" from the immanent history of consciousness, whereas Merleau-Ponty opted for departing from an intersubjective and corporeal incarnation, such as a historical situation, that modified everything.

Just as the evolutionary process of research is not cumulative and sequential, scientific studies on the simulation between perception and action have been interrupted, starting with the diffusion of studies on neurophysiology carried out by C. S. Sherrington (1918) and later by the great impact of the theory and form known as Gestalt (Gibson 1966) and the theory of constructivism (Piaget 1971). These two theorists (James J. Gibson and Jean Piaget) recognized action and perception as two connected but distinct instances, one occurring after the other. So it was not the same idea as the simulation proposed by the research in the cognitive sciences that preceded it, but rather one that seemed more in tune with the current discussion.

There is no doubt that Merleau-Ponty's statement—that every theory of the body is already one of perception—remains essential. In the meantime, the explanations became radicalized to the extent that the notion of time changed. So it has become plausible today to claim that perceiving is already a form of action. Alva Noë (2004) makes clear how perception is not something that happens for us or in us. It is something that we do. What we perceive is determined by what we do, what we know how to do, and what we are ready to do. These actions are subtly different from one another, but intimately related.

To perceive is to test implicitly the effects of movement on sensory stimulation. The most central and important assertion that Noë makes is that there exists an enactive action[1] that would be the very ability to perceive, which is not only dependent on but also constituted by the fact of our having a certain type of sensorimotor knowledge. So only creatures with certain bodily abilities can be perceptive beings the same way we are. One's own movement depends on the modes of perception of one's consciousness. But both self-perception and perspective self-consciousness are abilities that relate us not only with our own organism, but with our surroundings.

Another important aspect of the enactive approach is the rejection of the idea that perception is somehow a process that happens in the brain, where a perceptual system constructs an internal representation of the world. Undoubtedly, perception depends on what happens in the brain, which organizes an uninterrupted flow of internal representations. As such, it is important to note that perception is not a process that is concentrated solely there in the brain, but a kind of activity in the animal as a whole.

This explanation is rather different from others such as that of Susan Hurley, who in 1998 proposed a relationship between perception and action as a kind of input and output. Her hypothesis was very well received and to this day enjoys a considerable amount of recognition. For Hurley, perception is a stimulus from the world to the mind, whereas action is a stimulus from the mind to the world. In this case, thought can be understood as a process of mediation.

Noë considers this divorce between perception and action dangerous and inadequate. According to him, thought cannot be considered a mediation between one thing and another. Perception is intrinsically a thought. The case of blindness is often cited as being exemplary in many ways, both in his work and in that of other authors. Blind creatures are able to think, but those incapable of thinking are unable to look, that is, to perceive anything visually. Perception and perceptive consciousness are both cognitive activities. There is always the assumption that the blind live a life of "incompleteness." However, long-term blindness (congenital, for example) has nothing to do with rupture or incompleteness of the cognitive process. A blind person does not experience blindness as a lack.

The basis of perception is an implicit practical knowledge of the ways that movement carries out changes in stimulation. When someone puts on glasses or distorted lenses, for example, the patterns of dependency between movement and stimulation are altered. Eye and head movement lead to anticipated changes in sensory stimulation, and the result is not "seeing differently," but failing to see. Gaps are created between the perception of vision and the act of seeing itself, and that is why one cannot see.

Many of the most important scientists who have studied vision and perception have argued that living beings construct an internal model in order to perceive the world. Noë claims that vision is not a process through which the brain constructs a detailed internal model of representation. That doesn't mean that representation doesn't exist, but that the notion of representation needs to be reconsidered. He gives the example of the tourist in a foreign city who wants to go to a castle. The first option would be to buy a map and follow it step by step until arriving at the desired location. The second option would be that in which, from where one is standing, it is already possible to see the castle. In this case, there is no map, but the tourist intuitively follows the clues found along the way until arriving at the castle. There is not necessarily a map given a priori, but we intuit how to follow the clues.

So perceiving is not just having a sensation or receiving sensory impressions, but having sensations that someone understands. This entails a better understanding of what "someone understands" means and what "conceptual understanding" is.

There is no unanimity in this field. On the contrary, it concerns a rather polemical topic that needs to be studied carefully. For Noë, who sees it differently than other authors, the basis of understanding is always conceptual. This hypothesis is somewhat peculiar because it implies a recognition that a large part of perceptual content is conceptual, when it is generally accepted that to formulate a concept implies being able to make judgments, something that would correspond to a subsequent stage.

Judgments always look for some kind of truth, and the laws of truth are normally considered logical. In order to understand them, it is necessary to approach the distinction between the way things are and the way they appear to be. Humans and nonlinguistic beings alike perceive, although the latter are mostly unable to carry out intellectual practices. Noë admits that other animals and human infants perceive, but they do not need concepts in order to perceive. This is important in order for us to understand that he is not saying that it is all the same thing. There is clearly a difference between perceiving, conceptualizing, and judging; all the same, what Noë makes clear is that these differences are not the same ones invoked by common sense. Perception is not something that comes before conceptualization; it is already cognitive in the sense that it is a sensorimotor ability from which protoconcepts emerge.[2]

Sometimes we need categories in order to perceive, but we do not have individual concepts regarding perception. Noë proposes that sensorimotor ability is already a conceptual ability in and of itself. In this sense, movement would essentially be cognitive because the way we understand how things happen is always in sensorimotor terms. It is in this same way that we represent the properties given to us.

At this point, there is an important aspect that needs to be highlighted. If sensorimotor abilities are already a type of simple concept (or protoconcept) even before involving what one normally understands as judgment, then perceptive experience would already be, in this rather primary instance, inseparable from conceptual understanding. In this way, the supposedly nonconceptual character of experiences would become increasingly unsatisfactory.

What Noë is suggesting is that perceiving is already a way of thinking about the world, or, in other words, that all experience, even without being configured as judgment, is thinkable. To have an experience is to be confronted with a possible way of the world, and the content of experience and the content of thought are one and the same.

Another important aspect is that the primary act of relating is always in the possibility of action. One doesn't "apply" sensorimotor knowledge to experience. It is tested continually *as experience*. Perceptual experience is a way of exploring the world. The necessary abilities are sensorimotor and conceptual at the same time. In philosophy, from Plato to Henri Bergson, the idea of concept involves articulation, cutting, and overlaying. A concept is a whole because it presents a way of totalizing the components, but it's a fragmented whole. According to Gilles Deleuze, it is only under that condition that one can exit mental chaos. In a panoramic flight over these philosophical theories it seems their understandings are in tune with one another, but there are subtleties that merit mention, especially concerning the work of Deleuze and Félix Guattari, who also dedicated themselves to thinking specifically about the nature of concepts, proposing some preliminary bridges with science and art.

For these authors, "the concept is an incorporeal one, although it is embodied or goes into effect in bodies" (1997, 33). Here one has to be a bit careful in order to understand what that means. In *Vocabulaire de Gilles Deleuze* (2003), there is a whole explanation on the way in which the notion of concept in Deleuze appears in his different works. A concept is never confused with the state of things in which it takes effect. It is an act of thought that operates with infinite velocity. Concepts, according to Deleuze, are to philosophy (as a multiplicity and not general or abstract ideas) what the prospectus is to science (as propositions and not judgments), and what precepts and affect are to art (and thus should not be confused with perceptions and feelings). These observations show how language, in the way it is understood by Deleuze, is always subjected to "incomparable uses" (for example, in the areas of philosophy, science, and art). But it is good to note that these "uses" do not define the difference among the disciplines without also constituting their intersections.

In *What Is Philosophy?* (Deleuze and Guattari 1992), "the concept enunciates the happening, not being or the thing itself." So it is a pure happening, a haecceity, an entity: the happening of another, or the happening of the face when taken as a concept. A bird, as the authors explain, can also be a happening. Therefore, it is important to observe that the notion of "incorporeal" does not exactly imply the absence of the *body*. The concept is defined by the "inseparability of a finite number of heterogeneous components passed at one point of absolute flyover at infinite velocity" (1992, 33). That is why the philosophical concept does not refer to what is lived by way of compensation, "but consists of erecting a happening that flies over all of what is lived, as well as any state of things. Each concept cuts out the happening and reshapes it in its own way" (1992, 47).

When perception is seen from this angle, there are three recognizable planes that are as irreducible as their elements: the plane of immanence in philosophy, the plane of composition in art, and the plane of reference in science, each identified respectively as a form of concept, a force of sensation, and a function of knowing. The problems of interference among these planes, according to Deleuze and Guattari, come together in the brain (1992, 277). They make up a dynamic network, which means that knowing is not a form or a force, but a function.

Studying perception as cognition starting from Noë, we find that the relationship with the world via thought/experience differs not in type, but in degree. The most primitive degree (the one that starts off the process) is not defined as sensory qualities or intensities, but as a sensorimotor understanding. The ability to think about the world would also be (and in an indiscernible way) our ability to experience it. From this perspective, experience is an aptitude implemented in action that translates the different connections between an organism and its surroundings, which, in turn, are configured not as separated instances (inside and outside) but, indeed, as systems that coevolve.

Based on the studies of Noë (for whom concepts are already sensorimotor abilities), Berthoz (who recognizes movement as a sixth sense fundamental to perception, simulated action), and Mark Johnson (who also identifies conceptual capacity as dependent on sensorimotor processes), we find that the different planes (immanence, composition, and reference) exist in a gray area that can be defined as a way of being in motion and, consequently, being alive.

From here forward, we will study in greater detail some of our cognitive abilities in order to better understand how, simply by our simultaneously analyzing different levels of description of the same phenomenon, everything can change. I propose beginning with empathy and with feelings, which have, in an evolutionary sense, presented themselves as some of the principal profaning actions of our organism, calling into question Enlightenment ideas of identity and individuality, ones that at times still provide direction to some theories, especially in the field of the so-called human sciences.

## Mirror Neurons

Is it possible to "open" the body to the experience of the Other even before the formulation of language, a logical discourse of rationalization and judgments? Research on the so-called mirror neurons has helped respond to this question, explaining how the phenomenon of empathy arises.

The study began with the experiments of Giacomo Rizzolatti, first published in the 1980s in specialized journals such as *Experimental Brain Research* (1981, 1982, 1987, 1988) and *Brain* (1983), until he finally released a book with coauthor Corrado Sinigaglia, *Mirrors in the Brain: How Our Minds Share Actions and Emotions* (2006; Eng. trans. 2008), which shared with a broader audience his discovery of mirror neurons in the premotor ventral area of primates. At first, Rizzolatti and Arbib (1998) confirmed the relevance of these neurons for studies of language, but gradually the research began to unfold. The experiments showed that when the primates completed certain actions, specific neurons were activated, but when one primate observed another eating peanuts, its neurons became activated as well. So internally a landscape was configured as if one were, in fact, in the place of the other. Rizzolatti noted that these same neurons were responsible for the imitation of gestures and vocalizations. The premotor area in question could be considered homologous to the region of the brain called Broca's area, which is associated with expressive and syntactic aspects of language in humans.

Another aspect of mirror neurons that has been researched is related to the capacity for judgment and evaluation, an aspect already present, as we have seen, in discussions about perception. Patients with anosognosia—a deficit of self-awareness in which a patient with a certain condition is not aware of having it—typically have a stroke in the right hemisphere of the brain, which paralyzes the left side of the body, rendering them incapable of moving their bodies on that side. Despite being lucid and intelligent, they do not seem conscious of the problem and usually consider themselves to be absolutely normal. When observing other patients with the same pathology, they are also incapable of recognizing the problem in others because they would need to have the mirror neurons functioning perfectly in order to evaluate the observed image.

So in order to judge the movement of others, it would be necessary to create a simulation (an internal virtual reality) that corresponded to the movements of one's own brain. Without mirror neurons it is impossible to organize this kind of simulation. Simulated reality is what makes it possible to recognize the reality of what is going on outside of the body.

This became a key issue proposed by Vittorio Gallese and Alvin Goldman (1998) in order to do an initial reading of another's behavior. That means that the simulation of what is going on outside of the body is not simply that of the newest experiences of the virtual world of video games or other technological apparatuses; it also says something about the way that we communicate, perceive, and know what is around us.

The organism presents its own solutions as far as otherness is concerned. It is in this way that the emotion of sympathy can be transformed into the feeling of empathy or, rather, the feeling "as if it were the body of the other." It has to do with a virtual corporeal loop, as António Damásio suggests (2003), an internal simulation that occurs in the brain and consists of a rapid change in the mapping of the body. This simulation occurs when certain regions of the brain such as the prefrontal and premotor cortices send signals directly to the somatosensory regions. The neurons able to do that are in the prefrontal cortex in both primates and human beings, and it is not for nothing that they were named mirror neurons. They simulate internally the movement that other organisms make in their field of vision, allowing for a preview of movements that might become necessary for communication with the individual whose movements are "mirrored." So the mechanism of empathy emerges from actions on the part of these neurons. The simulation of bodily states in somatosensory regions is the momentary creation of a series of maps of the body that do not correspond to the current reality of that body. The brain utilizes signals that have come from the body in order to sculpt a particular state as if these signals were nothing more than clay. What we feel in those moments is based on a false construct and not on the "true" state of the body.

Among all the possibilities of simulation of bodily states that do not actually exist, in the history of evolution there have been many cases of hallucination. For some time, the brain would have simply been able to produce true maps of corporeal states. Later, possibilities emerged such as the temporary elimination of mappings related to pain, or the opposite: mapping fictional states of pain. There is evidence that some of these strategies remained registered in the genome, that the brain can produce modifications of the maps of the body very rapidly in a time frame of hundredths of milliseconds or even less, which would correspond only to the time of transmission of signals from the region of the prefrontal cortex to the nearby somatosensory regions.

Some auditory and visual hallucinations are disruptive and do not contribute to evolutionary strategies of survival, as is the case with hallucinations observed in people with neurological disorders. Those of smell and taste, typical of epileptics, are also usually quite complex and destabilizing.

Other ways of interfering in the construction of maps of the body are molecular mechanisms that result from the introduction of drugs into the system that alter feelings, as in the case with depression. If Damásio's hypothesis is correct that feelings have their origins in neural patterns that map out the most varied aspects of the state of the body, then chemical substances that alter our mood can change activity patterns of somatosensory regions. This depends on three different mechanisms that either work separately or in tandem: the mechanism that interferes in the transmission of signals coming from the body, the one in charge of creating a particular activity pattern inside of the maps of the body, and the third, which would act by way of a change in the state of the body itself.

Since the discovery of mirror neurons, there has also been research on to what extent they could be responsible for imitation. In order to get there, it is first and foremost necessary to understand what imitation is. From a neurophysiological point of view, there are at least two options: the first was developed by experimental psychologists and suggests that imitating says something about reproducing an act that belongs in some way to what is called the individual's motor heritage. The second, proposed by ethologists, supposes that through observation an individual learns a new pattern of action and is able to reproduce it in detail.

The two views are related to what is called the problem of correspondence, or how we can carry out an analogous action to the one we perceive. The system of vision utilizes certain parameters of codification different from those of the system of movement, and the first question has to do with which cortical processes are involved and what sensorimotor transformations are necessary. At this point, important questions arise: How can we acquire new capabilities for action? How can we translate the vision of a series of meaningless movements so as to allow for actions that are meaningful for us?

The first form of imitation presented a separation between sensory and motor codes. In this case, imitation is possible because of associative processes that unite elements that do not have anything in common a priori.

In the second case, the observed action and the one carried out share the same neural code and would be a condition for imitation to happen. In recent years, this second option has been the more accepted one, and it is important to note that such investigations already had important precedents in the research by Alain Berthoz mentioned earlier in this chapter.

So since the nineteenth century, there have long been indications that perception and execution of actions are part of the same representational schema. The discovery of mirror neurons, however, suggests a requalification of principles; that is to say, the common representational schema is no longer considered an abstract representational schema but rather seen as a transformative mechanism: for example, from pieces of visual information into potential motor acts.

As has been known for over a century, there are different areas of the brain. For a long time, scholars thought that Area 46 was responsible for the recombination of each of the motor acts with a definition of a new pattern of action that would be as similar as possible to the one given as an example, that is, like a kind of working memory. More recently, the analysis of forms of imitation revealed that they always depend on the cortical zones endowed with mirror properties.

So it has nothing to do with a repertory or motor heritage. That would not be sufficient to explain the process of imitation and learning. The mere presence of mirror neurons would also not be enough, although it has been shown to be a necessary condition alongside other cortical regions.

As far as human beings are concerned, this ability exists from early on. There may not be a mirror in a baby's crib, but even so, newborns are able to imitate their parents; that is, even without seeing the gesture made by their own body, they are able to imitate. Darwin had already studied the phenomenon of motor resonance, observing that when an athlete jumps, the spectators move their feet regardless of whether they see themselves making the action with their own bodies. Nevertheless, with the discovery of mirror neurons, it is possible to perceive different modes of communication, establishing a rather peculiar connection between one subject and another. It is this communication through resonance that would also characterize the relationship between other animals, not just humans. Learning by imitation integrates different processes: that which permits the observer to segment the action into each of the elements that it comprises (sequences of acts already tested previously), and others that should permit the motor acts to be codified in such a way that the action reflects that of the one who has demonstrated it (the one who acted first).

Thus, one can clearly see that mirror neurons make possible the emergence of a shared space that is, in turn, a space of action. There are also two different moments: while it is one thing to understand an action, being able to imitate it is something else entirely. There is an increasingly accepted hypothesis that processes of production and perception are related and that the representation of both processes are to some extent the same.

From these studies, it becomes all the more urgent to rethink the notions of communication and translation. When we perceive the first movements of others, these movements already tell us something about the very nature of the act, that is to say, the communication of communicability and not of a specific meaning,[3] which would already be another subsequent process of organization of conventions and other metaphorical networks of displacements. Crossing different levels of representation and communication, we find evidence that it was the progressive evolution of the system of mirror neurons that originated the recognition of acts and inter-individual forms of communication, which in turn made the first translations of the image of the Other possible. According to Gerald Edelman (2001), communication and learning emerge in the process of evolution well before primary consciousness. It was the mirror neurons that allowed for the experience of otherness and empathy as basic preconditions for the understanding of all communicative action.

## Feelings

Besides empathy, another recurrent theme that refers to relations of otherness is that of feelings. The essential contents of feelings are nothing more than the configurations of the bodily state that the somatosensory maps represent. Feeling of pain and pleasure are, according to Damásio, the scaffolding of the mind. In this way, the transitory maps of the body transform rapidly by way of mutual and reverberative influences of the brain and the body whenever feelings occur. The positive or negative value given to feelings and their intensity are aligned with matters always concerning the regulation of life.

If the earlier explanation of the modes of organization of feeling in the brain and its connections with the body made it seem that it was ultimately a matter of a dichotomy between body and mind, now is the time to put it all back together again to make clear how the attributes of the body and the mind constitute a sole substance. One of the ways to do that could be through calling it Mark Johnson's proposed naming of ecological organism (to be discussed in the next chapter); the Other would be Damásio's reading of the philosopher Baruch Spinoza (1632–77), for whom the human mind was already considered "the body's idea," and for whom the fundamental key to understanding the mind is found in the theory of affect. It is particularly the second of these two possibilities that is of interest to us at the moment, seeing as it points toward the recognition of feeling as a powerful resistance strategy for the organism.

Damásio understands that the notion of affect elaborated by Spinoza can help relate emotions to feelings and that these, in turn, are associated with transitions in the states of the organism that ensure its life, but can also sacrifice it, bearing in mind the ambivalence that is also part of the process (body and mind in a continuum).

Before properly explaining the modes of organization of feelings, Damásio (2003, 51–53) proposes a classification of emotions that, in his opinion, is a necessary evil from a didactic perspective. They are of three types, starting with the basic emotions, defined as manifestations of the regulatory reactions of the organism, almost always described in terms of well-being and discomfort. As for primary emotions, the second category, the most studied emotions include fear, anger, disgust, surprise, sadness, and happiness. The circumstances that cause these primary emotions and the behaviors that define them are fairly consistent across various cultures and species. And the third type, social emotions, would be sympathy, compassion, embarrassment, shame, guilt, pride, jealousy, envy, gratitude, admiration, amazement, indignation, and contempt. Basic and primary emotions make up part of those social emotions. Connections vary, but all these emotions are related, without exception, to adaptive corrections of the states of the body, which lead to changes in the brain mappings of those bodily states; these mappings are the feelings.

Starting out from Spinoza's theory of affect, Damásio goes on to explain that joy (*laetitia*) is associated with a transition of the organism to a state of greater functional harmony and indicates an "increased freedom of action." Nonetheless, this "map of joy" (or feeling of joy) can be falsified by using drugs, for example, and does not necessarily reflect a current state of the organism. The problem is that sooner or later, this improvement will not be biologically sustainable and will serve as a prelude to the very degradation of biological functions.

There is some controversy in the translation of the terms proposed by Spinoza. *Laetitia* was translated as joy or exultation, but other authors gave it different names, such as Amélie Rorty (1991), who chose to translate it as pleasure. Damásio considers pleasure to be a rather particular feeling, and in some ways more primary. If it is possible to say it, the feelings of pain and pleasure are more primary than those of joy and sadness. According to Damásio, *tristitia* would be sadness or regret, but it can also be taken to mean fear or anger (2003, 321). As far as the organism is concerned, each state has singularities that are often more specific than words can describe, and one state cannot be confused with another, unfolding into distinct possibilities.

In this way, each feeling-map seems to engender adaptive responses in the form of bodily states, and vice versa. The maps of grief (or feelings of grief), for example, are associated with functional imbalance. The ease of action is reduced. These maps are not infrequently associated with the presence of pain, signs of illness, or physiological disagreement, indicating a diminished coordination of vital functions. If the grief is not remedied, illness and death will follow.

These maps of grief and pain almost always reflect the real state of the organism; no one abuses drugs that lead to depression. According to Spinoza, the notion of *tristitia* leads to the transition of the organism into a state of disharmony. Power and freedom of action are reduced. The person is invaded by sadness and separated from their *conatus*, which is the natural tendency for self-preservation. This appears in those feelings that result from severe depression where there is a risk of suicide. The endocrine and immune systems participate in chronic depression as if a pathogenic agent (bacteria or virus) had invaded the organism. But not every negative feeling is in fact destructive of harmony. Sometimes these feelings are defense strategies such as appropriately directed anger, which can help avoid potential abuse, or fear, which can prevent exposure to possible threats.

For this reason, Damásio clarifies that feelings are mental sensors on the inside of the body, true witnesses to our state of life. These are the mental manifestations of balance and harmony as well as disharmony and disagreement.

When all of this is linked to social practice, the very question of communication needs to be rethought. As we have experience, we organize different categories of social situations. Our knowledge includes: (1) facts related to problems that we can't deal with and need to resolve; (2) the option we choose for resolving them; (3) the factual result of this solution; and (4) the result of the solution in terms of emotion and feeling, punishment or reward. The difficulty in seeing the future caused by frontal lesions, as in the case cited by Damásio in *Descartes' Error* (1994), is similar to the situation of drug addicts and alcoholics. That is because the mapping of the body is systematically false.

One of the most interesting issues that emerges from Damásio's explanations is that problems and solutions can be wrong, but in bodily terms they are always real, and this fact affects our lives in innumerable ways. Ethical behaviors, for example, constitute a subset of social behaviors and have everything to do with emotions and feelings. To discuss this, it has become evident, especially in ethology studies over the last twenty-five years or so, that it is not only the human species that can claim ethical behavior. There are experiments that reveal ethical behavior in crows and in some mammals such as bats, wolves, and chimpanzees. Among these species there is sympathy, attachment, embarrassment, shame, pride, and submission. There is also punishment and reward. Vampire bats, for example, detect their cheating peers and are capable of inflicting severe punishment; crows do the same. Rhesus monkeys have even more sophisticated and altruistic behavior.

Marc Hauser (1996 and 2006) has conducted experiments that show how some monkeys prefer to go days without food to avoid pulling a chain that would give their companion an electric shock. In this context, ethics is nothing more than biological regulation that includes the production of feelings and emotions. Evolution provided mechanisms that set off certain emotions that lead to problem solving and opportunities. The extent to which its devices are in tune with one another depends on the organism, the environment, and coevolutionary history, which is organized based on the alliance between nature and culture. William James imagined that feelings were a perception of bodily states when the body is modified by emotion. One of his well-known phrases suggests that we don't cry because we are sad; we become sad because we are crying. In this same context, it is important to remember that according to Damásio, feelings have their origins not always in real states of the body, but rather in the real state of the brain maps that the somatosensory regions of the brain construct at all times. Once again, it all has to do with a problem of representation in the mind/body continuum. If we start at this level of description, everything becomes more complex, from the most intimate relationships of the body with the environment. What can one say, then, of the social implications of these phenomena?

Perhaps the most fundamental role of feelings as they pertain to ethics has been to maintain the condition of life in such a way that it could play a leading role in organizing behavior. It is precisely because feelings continue to play this role that they need to be heard when it comes to socio-politically organizing the instances of society. Studying feelings more closely, we find it ever clearer that in the body, fiction and truth are absolutely real. It is the operation of translation that announces and embodies both boundaries and gray areas.

# 4

# Circuits of Activation

## Signifying Desire

After more than thirty years of reflection, Mark Johnson (2008) came to the conclusion that people want their lives to be meaningful, but little is known about what meaning is or why it is always corporeal. In the United States, the pragmatist John Dewey was one of the first to recognize that there was no way to reflect seriously on the meaning of life and thought without studying aesthetics and the body.

He was an exception, considering that for many years aesthetics was treated as something of lesser importance, with no relation either to cognition or to the nature of the mind. According to Johnson, the ideas that led to this sort of conclusion were supported by assumptions such as: the mind is disembodied, thought transcends feeling, feelings are not part of meaning or knowledge, aesthetics is concerned solely with questions of subjective taste, and finally, art is a luxury, not a condition for humanity to flourish.

In his view, aesthetics would be just as important for the study of meaning because meaning is always more than words and deeper than concepts. Thus, in order to begin studying the emergence of the act of signifying, it is important to recognize that the mind and body are not two separate things, but aspects of a single organic process. Meaning, thought, and language emerge from the aesthetic dimensions of bodily activities and are inseparable both from the images and patterns of sensorimotor processes and from emotions.

The problems that revolve around this form of reasoning are numerous and complex. There is a proliferation of dualities that permeate the mind/body dichotomy, such as cognition/emotion, fact/value, knowledge/imagination, thought/feeling.

However, the body is always interacting with aspects of the environment in a process of exchange of experience. For this reason, what we call body and mind, Johnson explains, are abstract aspects of the flow between organism and environment, given that the notion of organism involves body and mind inseparably. This is easily verified when one considers that when any functional problem is faced in the relationship, the ability to experience is lost.

The recognition that meaning is rooted in bodily experience further implies the recognition that imaginative as well as conceptual capacity are dependent on our sensorimotor capacities. That is why what we usually call reason is neither a concrete nor an abstract thing, but rather embodied processes through which our experiences are explored, critiqued, and transformed into questions.

Reason cannot be considered a preestablished fact or capacity, and imagination is embodied in this way in corporeal processes, creating and transforming experiences all the time. The emergence of newness refers to new connective possibilities of preexisting patterns, qualities, and feelings. There is not, in this sense, any kind of radical freedom, nor a subject capable of making choices freely. David Hume, William James, and António Damásio have discussed this issue at different times, and all of them were interested in understanding how the body assumes meaning and what the notion of embodied thought means for life.

As has been explained, there is a close connection between life and movement. Movement is one of the conditions for sensing how the world is and who we are. Knowledge comes from movement, that of the body as much as that of the moving objects that are part of our surroundings. So movement is one of the main ways we learn the meaning of things, and a good part of what we learn is processed by what George Lakoff and Mark Johnson (1999) called the cognitive unconscious.

Another fundamental topic, mentioned in the third chapter, is that of emotion and of feeling, which is at the heart of our capacity to experience meanings. In this sense, Johnson says, William James, much as Charles Sanders Peirce before him, pointed out that someone's experience of hesitation is always aided by a corporeal tension and by some kind of restraint. The body does not accompany doubt. It is doubt. Meaning emerges precisely from the bodily experience of blocking the flow of experience in the direction of new thoughts and feelings. Dewey collaborated in this discussion to the extent that he explained how the location of emotions are "situations," and not bodies and minds.

Despite these considerations, in much of the bibliography on the topic, meaning is still considered a linguistic phenomenon. Even in what it says regarding artistic experiences that propose other modes of representing the body and its surroundings, little is discussed about how we experience and understand art beyond the analogy between art and language.

For years it has been taken for granted that art is necessarily a language. The metaphor of phrases and sentences, grammar, and syntax was broadly utilized to talk about painting, dance, music, and so on. When Johnson brought aesthetics into the center of what a human being means, he was aided by two propositions. The first claims that aesthetics is not merely a theory of art but must be seen more broadly, as a possible way of studying how humans create and experience meanings; and the second shows that just because the process of embodying meaning in art is the same as that which makes linguistic meaning possible, it doesn't mean that art necessarily has to be subjugated to linguistic meaning.

Johnson considers the seventeenth and eighteenth centuries to be largely responsible for some of the conclusions that to this day are respected and disseminated by common sense. This is because at that time, that the so-called faculties or powers of the mind were formulated: faculties such as sensation, feeling, imagination, understanding, and reason. Such faculties were divided into higher and lower. Everything that was supposedly intellectual or cognitive was considered one of the higher faculties, whereas the lower faculties were those of the body and as such not cognitive, but only subjective. In this context, beauty would primarily be a matter of feeling and not of thinking.

Johnson explains that Immanuel Kant's work *The Critique of Judgment* (1790) unfortunately assisted in deepening the dichotomy between cognitive and noncognitive acts, despite having added the importance of imagination and its role in remaking reality. Above all, because of subsequent rereadings of Kant, in the eyes of many of his commentators, aesthetics ended up being definitively reduced to feeling, excluding cognition from the field of art.

In the twentieth century, studies emerged that began to question such compartmentalizations of cognitive and perceptive acts. In addition to Dewey's proposals, especially in his book *Art as Experience* (1934), other studies questioned the relationship between thought and feeling. In the field of art history, it was Rudolf Arnheim in his work *Visual Thinking* (1969) who affirmed that thought was not an exclusive privilege of mental processes, but rather the ingredient of one's own perception.

Johnson took up this topic once again, departing from the discussion of meanings, which were, in his view, a matter of relationships and connections rooted in the relationship between organism and environment. What one usually calls "the meaning of something" is always in its current and potential relationships. As part of pragmatism, this appears formulated as a matter of how to connect what is happening now to what came before and what already presents itself as future experience. Johnson elucidates that feelings are not just felt; they also make sense and build meanings. What is defined as the mind emerges from the sharing of meanings. That is why meaning is corporeal and social at the same time, given that it does not exist without communicative interaction. What seems important to make clear here is that meaning is always relational. What we emphasize and what we ignore will make all the difference in perceiving what something, someone, or a given situation means. So it seems more appropriate, instead of discussing the mind/body dichotomy, to use the term *ecological organism*, which would include body, brain, and environment. Human life could be understood as the art of giving meaning to our bodily experiences. If this does not guarantee us permanence as we face the high rate of mortality of symbolic systems, at least it will allow us to avoid the condition of the *Muselmann*, exhausted by the anticipation of death while still alive.

## The Presence of the Body and the Emergence of Microcommunications

One way to understand the processes of translation and meaning is related to what is often called "presence of the body." According to André Lepecki (2004), it was only after the impact of the concept of *Dasein* conceived by Martin Heidegger, Michel Foucault's criticism of regimentation techniques, and Gilles Deleuze and Félix Guattari's rereadings of the "Body without Organs" (BwO), first proposed by Antonin Artaud, that body and presence radically destabilized the epistemological basis on which art was built. From there, these concepts became recurrent in debates and were expanded by new discussions, such as in the work of Jacques Derrida, as his "metaphysics of presence" and the notion of "trace" significantly increased his importance. For Derrida, the metaphysics of presence could be understood as a demanding, potent, systematic, and inexpressible desire for meaning (1973, 60). Or, as Eric Landowski (1997) explained, the mode of presence in the world would still be a unique form of sensitive attention, a total availability, an immediate agreement with the things and people around or the small happenings chained to one another, which, in this manner, built their own plot of a narrative with no other concern than that of the coming instant. In this sense, the spatialization (or the action of space) would also be a form of presentification (action of presence).

I do not intend right now to present a survey of every approach that has sought to explain, define, or simply call attention to the body's presence. To some extent, this term has already been discussed with sufficient breadth by the aforementioned authors. Keeping in mind the discussions I have presented so far, I propose to delve further into two ideas that to me seem fundamental and related to what I have called circuits of the body's activation. As such, I am bringing to the discussion bibliographies constructed by Japanese researchers, rarely cited in Western research.

To begin, I consider bodily presence to be what gives visibility to thought, so it is becoming increasingly valuable in contemporary art experiments, the objectives of which have primarily been to expose thoughts, as opposed to products or aesthetic results to be rapidly consumed.[1] If we take this idea as a starting point, we will find that it is intimately related to the exposure of the gaze and to the displacements arising from this very exposure. This issue has been researched for more than three centuries by Japanese culture based on the concepts of *mitate-e* (further discussed below) and *fûdo* (a kind of mental environment of immovability or stillness). In addition, I propose to identify the body's presence through what from here on I will call "interface micromovements," that is, the movements that are organized in the passage between the inside and outside of the body. This is because it is precisely during this passage that they can gain visibility, in the interstitial moment when they begin to make themselves known but often are still not clearly recognizable.

In order to discuss the relationship between bodily presence, visibility of thought, and interface micromovements, one must shift a few beliefs in their clichés, beginning with the very concept of image and autonomy of vision. From a cognitive point of view, image is not restricted to what is seen, and, in turn, vision is not separate from the other bodily senses, constantly being completed and given new dimension by a complex network of perceptions. According to Shigehisa Kuriyama (1999), presence is nothing more than a certain tone of muscle that is pronounced at the moment in which one body is exposed to the gaze of the other, eliciting countless displacements. Augustin Berque (1993, 45–48) identifies this "instituting gaze" with the notion of *mitate-e*, a kind of renewal of form through the displacement of an image, movement, or diagram present in another experience that becomes transported to the present situation. In other words, it is a kind of "seeing-as" that can be understood not as imitation but as the expression of a proper meaning from another reference: its value is derived from its reference to the other.

For example, based on this strategy, transfers of foreign urban models took place on Japanese land and from there were claimed as entirely Japanese experiments rather than "emblems of foreign urbanization." Another example is Kabuki theater, recalled by Masakatsu Gunji (1985). *Mitate-e*, in this case, is an offshoot of the concept of *yatsushi*, established in the Edo period (1603–1867), and is essentially an attempt to modernize everything, translating into terms of contemporary society what had been attempted before in other situations. In Kabuki, this happens regularly when situations, images, and gestures from, for instance, Chinese literature are performed in the theatrical scene as a game that works with "double identity and double meaning" (Gunji 1985, 16–17).

The notion of bodily presence would be one of the moments of this translation-displacement, in which something manifests (an action, an idea, an image) and gains visibility, establishing a new process of communication with its surroundings (audience and context).

The way that this process takes place can be understood from another Japanese concept: *fûdosei*. Tetsurô Watsuji (2005) defined *fûdosei* as "the structural moment of human existence." For Watsuji, the human being is made of two halves, one being its animal (individual) body and the other the medial (collective) body. This back and forth between private and public, individual and collective is always present in the organization of *fûdosei*, which could be translated as a kind of *environmentalization*, that is, environmental action (climate, landscape, symbolic universes, etc.) as a structural element of human existence. Watsuji's research ended up being interpreted as a response to the Heideggerian investigation revealed in *Being and Time*, where, as previously mentioned, Heidegger defined *Dasein* as being-towards-death. Watsuji read the book and began to discuss "being-towards-life." This is because from his point of view, as Berque (2009) explains,[2] it had to do not only with discussing temporality, but with identifying how temporality and spatiality, as well as historicity and regionality, corresponded. In this case, the body's presence would be the body's flesh, but also its connections not only with different objects, but with multiple realities, that is, a flow of not only individual but eminently collective information. Everything would be related in the supposed present moment, without any separation between nature and culture: climate, landscape, the tempera-

tures of the body and the environment, the spatiality of the body and its surroundings, history and the material/symbolic situation of the here and now
(regionality).

As mentioned in the third chapter, in terms of perception (and specifically
the perception of the Other), at the moment information comes from the outside, sensations are always placed "in relation to," creating connections. So this
is how the imaginative process is organized, and when it starts it no longer
distinguishes between what comes from within and what comes from without.
The history of the body in movement is also the history of imagined movement,
which embodies itself in action. Different bodily states modify the way information will be processed. State of mind is nothing more than a category of
functional states or sensorimotor images. In other words, state of mind is not
separate, nor is it anything other than representations (true or fictitious) of the
body's state.

These states are generated constantly and are not necessarily visible. Thus,
previously cited researchers like António Damásio, Alain Berthoz, George
Lakoff, Mark Johnson, and Alva Noë have explained that sensorimotor image is
not necessarily visual image but rather sensory actions that produce a functional bodily state. This occurs at the moment in which something is happening. When we pick up an object, for example, many changes are taking place at
the same time. William James (1890) had already proposed that the production
of movement is always guided by a sensation and that the generation of movement is the response to the sensory key. So while the motor actions are similar,
there is always a huge difference between picking up a cup and picking up a
machine gun. The mediations and organization of the metaphors of thought
radically change.

As I explained in my other book (Greiner 2005), it was Rodolfo Llinás
(2002) who emphasized that movement is always created from an oscillation,
a rhythmic event (as from a pendulum or a metronome) that is processed in
a neuron-like electric activity and manifests itself at the exact moment the
voltage crosses the membrane that envelops the cell. Potential actions are
messages that travel through axons (the prolongation of the nerve cell), forging the relationship between cerebral information and the body's peripheral
nerves. So the process always begins through a sensorimotor transformation.
Starting from changes in the present environment (where the action takes
place), movement is the guarantee of survival. The next step is what Llinás
calls "prediction." What he calls "self" would be understood, in this sense, as

the centralization of prediction, a kind of internal state that anticipates future possibility. This possibility is already movement and never appears outside of consciousness, but can be organized only when the body is on alert (a low level of consciousness). Llinás's principal hypothesis is that thought is the evolutionary internalization of movement.

In this sense, the presence of the body is nothing more than the externalization of a thought that comes from interface micromovements between the inside and outside of the body. Its recognition depends simultaneously on the "kinetic melody" composed in the body and the gaze of the other, which, in turn, engenders new displacements, reshaping interfaces and reinventing thoughts. It is for this reason that Berthoz considers movement our sixth sense (2001). Based on these studies, communication can no longer be restricted to the five senses related to our sense organs. Movement and the sensorimotor system are fundamental to communication.

Based on the issues raised in the first part of this book, which also called attention to the transit between the outside and inside, the private and the public, and their gray areas, one of the starting points to understanding how bodily presence can, and indeed does, organize itself as a political action is the recognition of the body's materiality. The subject is quite controversial. There is, even today, a tendency to think of the body's materiality as something strictly biological.

The philosopher Donn Welton, in the second volume of a series he organized about body and philosophy (*Body and Flesh: A Philosophical Reader*, 1998), presents what he called "contested and contesting constructions, the matrices and the flesh of culture." As part of this same publication, Susan Hekman prepared a dossier in which she presented a comparison between the work of Susan Bordo and Judith Butler, who have contributed to the debate around materiality and the so-called performativity of the body, deepening the notion of the body's presence and its political action. Bordo and Butler establish their epistemological foundation with Foucault's work as a starting point, although they differ greatly from each other. Apparently, both are interested in the formation of a field of feminist research, but some of the most important questions that underlie the debate are of interest when one is studying the recurring themes in this book, such as the nature/culture alliance and apparatuses of power.

Bordo claims that the body's materiality should be the center of feminist theory, while Butler believes that feminism should reject the metaphysical notions implicit in this discussion. According to Butler, although many studies are considered materialist, they in fact continue to insist on some dualities that, in turn, are fundamental to the discussion of bodily presence and its political unfoldings.

In 1985, Bordo asserted that the body, far from being fundamentally stable and acultural, was never a natural body. Just like everything constructed by humans, the body too should be recognized as a cultural construction and locus of social control. The practical rules by which the body is trained and modeled make it able to respond to the questions of social order. For Bordo, the body is not merely a material or "brutally biological" entity. Everything is culturally mediated and subject to interpretation and description. Starting with these assumptions, Bordo will study some illnesses known as predominantly feminine, such as hysteria and anorexia. She says that, observing these disorders, we see the body of the ill as an ideological construction emblematic of the definition of femininity of each period where they reemerged.

In her first works involving anorexia and bulimia, the author stated that these pathologies have never been explained by fact, medicine, or psychology, because they are "cultural illnesses" connected to the cultural codes of the Western woman's body. Bordo seems committed to studying the practical metaphysics of mind/body dualism. In *Unbearable Weight: Feminism, Western Culture, and the Body* (1993), her objective was to develop an effective political discourse on the feminine body. What appears unclear in her position is that the materiality of the body seems to be neither biological nor physical, although it performs these two realities. It is a cultural construction that resists definitions of the body in its materiality. Bordo says that materiality is a large umbrella encompassing many epistemological, political, and existential concepts and values. In broader terms, materiality would have to do with finality and relates to the inescapable localization in time and space, history and culture, that constantly pattern and limit us.

On the other hand, in *Subjects of Desire* (1987), Butler, like Bordo, identifies Foucault as a redirection of Western thinking on the body that would deepen the analyses of the other authors to follow him, such as Simone de Beauvoir, who defined the body as a historical idea and not a natural fact. But, slowly, Butler begins to develop a different relationship between history and materiality and, finally, will conclude in *Bodies That Matter* (1993) that materiality in itself has a history—the two are not separate. Therefore, in her view, the correct formulation would not exactly be that history inscribes or builds the body. The body's materiality already is, by its own nature, historical. It does not shelter or contain history. This history has no origin, beginning, middle, or end, but presents particular genealogies.

So Butler may say that social differences are not inseparable from discursive demarcations, which is not the same thing as claiming that discourse causes sexual difference, or that some kind of cultural determinism exists. Sex is a construction materialized through time. It is not a static condition, but a process. As such, "materialization" is never completed. Instabilities and rematerializations demarcate a domain in which force can turn against itself, especially when it comes to hegemonic forces. Butler continues throughout her work with a few fundamental questions: What is the materiality of a body, anyway? How does it communicate? Can it be claimed that the body's materiality is not the antecedent to discourse, but is, in fact, its effect? Or is it not, after all, a relationship of cause and effect?

In an attempt to reformulate the notion of the body's materiality, Butler proposes:

1. The body's material is inseparable from the regulatory norms that govern its materialization.
2. The understanding of performativity as reiterative power of discourse produces the phenomenon that regulates and restricts.
3. The construction of sex is no longer a bodily fact on which gender is artificially imposed, but a cultural norm that organizes the materialization of bodies.

Butler explains that the relationship between nature and culture assumed by some models of gender construction implies social agency. That is why she rejects the idea that everything is discourse and construction. If the subject is a construction, who is constructing it?

In common sense, this "construction" has been understood as being carried out by a subject, by a culture, or as a constructivism reduced to a determinism. However, in a closer reading of Foucault, one notices that there is no power that acts on something or someone, but rather a repeated act that, in its persistence and instability, is the power. The construction would not be, therefore, a solitary act or a causal process initiated by a subject and culminated in conjunction with fixed effects. The construction is a temporal process that operates through the reiteration of norms. In this sense, sex is both produced and destabilized over the course of its reiteration. Instability is the possibility of the deconstitution of the repetition process and can be recognized as the creation of a "productive crisis."

If we consider these ideas, offered so that we might reflect on what the presence of the body is and how it is presented, we can conclude that despite the diversity of experiences, some questions recur in its recognition. They are as follows:

- time-space displacements
- transitions from the instance of the private and individual to the public and collective
- the translation of a low level of description (micro) to the macroscopic sphere
- the alliance between nature and culture
- the ambivalence between instability and stability

As Michael S. Gazzaniga (2005) has explained, our brain has been producing a rather poor and precarious autobiography. We are not equipped to remember or faithfully represent anything that we see or perceive in the world. We are better at remembering what seems relevant to our survival, not all the details involved in different events. In this sense, according to the laws of nature, in order for a performance to ensure survival in its environment, it must make visible what is relevant in that moment. In a way, the mind/body continuum is always alert to the states of others. When presence gains visibility it allows us to understand once and for all that, in evolutionary terms, evolution is about saving the group and not only the individual person, because by saving the group, the person is also saved. For this to happen, new forms of life must be introduced.

## Rethinking Immaterial Labor

The dilemma between the materiality of the body and the immateriality of thinking has already been addressed by countless authors as a topic of debate, including in the field of gender and sexuality as we saw earlier. Nonetheless, what has been known as immaterial labor within recent discussions about capitalism and forms of life has to do with a related topic, albeit one that is not exactly the same. In this case, the focus is what is reproduced not as exploration/exploitation, but as subjectivities.

This concern seeks to rely on a certain vitality in capitalism. It is not distinguished from studies of the body, although it may not have absorbed some of the principal debates that, in my view, could give new dimension to important problems. Before we bridge them in greater detail, it is wise to point out a few aspects for those not familiar with this discussion.

The cycle of immaterial labor would be that which is capable of organizing work as an autonomous, thinking force and transforming it into a signifying experience, something that, according to Johnson, is part of the aptitudes of our ecological organisms but is not always achieved. In the work of Karl Marx, immaterial labor has been, in principle, set up in opposition to productive work. It had to do with labor that created no value, but that made value move more rapidly. Linked to intellectual capacity, it represented a metaphor that could help in understanding the passage between production and circulation.

The theories that discuss this topic today are a bit different than the theses set forth by Marx in the classic *Grundrisse der Kritik der politischen Ökonomie* (Fundamental Elements of the Critique of Political Economy, 1858), but they set out from related concerns. Authors such as Maurizio Lazzarato, Antonio Negri, and Paolo Virno investigate whether it is possible to go with a post-Fordist approach, one no longer based on the sale of products, but on another type of "production": the production of subjectivities.

The recent crises in labor value, then, should open up the possibility of establishing a social relationship that values cultural, artistic, cognitive, educational, and environmental activities, which would in turn constitute an alternative to the traditional rules of capitalism. What one sees in practice, however, is that such activities continue to have difficulty validating themselves in the face of market rules that have long been established and internalized. As Jesús Martín-Barbero (2003) explains, there is a constant threat of what is called employability. In chasing after employability, all kinds of concessions are made. In this way, mediation, autonomy, and legitimization should be the new categories of everyday life, able to transform the exclusively individual dimension into processes of collective production. This doesn't always happen, however.

Not without reason, the discussions on the differences between the people and the multitude became increasingly present in these debates. If the notion of a people goes back to Thomas Hobbes (1642) and is closely linked to the presence of a state, one that has concluded that the people is one and has a sole will, the notion of the multitude is from Baruch Spinoza (1677), who understood it as a form of political and social existence of the many as many.

This topic ends up being related, then, whether directly or indirectly, to the question of public and private. In this context, private (*privado*) doesn't just mean what is intimate and personal, related to a kind of interiority; it seems more directed toward what is deprived (*privado*) of a voice, of public presence. Domination, Martín-Barbero explains, inhabits language through assemblages of neutralization and shock absorption of the labor act contained in words. Not infrequently there is a culture of silence that attempts to demobilize, above all, words that generate meanings. In some cultures such as those of Latin America, silence and lack of communication became cultural heritage.

Furthermore, Paolo Virno (2004) identified how in liberal thought the multitude became a private dimension in such a way as to affect its presence in power games. The many are distanced from the sphere of common affairs. For that reason, the ways of understanding dichotomies such as public/private and individual/collective seem to have change. The multitude no longer opposes the individual, but rethinks it.

Another gray area, and one that is put in place with ever-greater efficiency as far as forms of labor and of life are concerned, is the one that erases the differences between anguish and fear. Virno contextualizes the topic, recalling how in Immanuel Kant (1790) there had been precise definitions of what they both were. Thus fear referred to a precise fact, an avalanche or losing one's job, while anguish doesn't have a precise cause. Heidegger (1927) used to say that mere exposure to the world could already provoke anguish, but among the multitudes of the contemporary world, explains Virno (2004, 65–67), the separation between fear and anguish appears definitively erased. The loss of a job, for example, is merged immediately with indeterminate anguish and a general disorientation that throws the subject into a gray area, where not only are the causes unclear, but fear becomes a public feeling and thus a matter for the many.

Bearing in mind all these questions, what about new modes of production? Marx spoke about a general intellect which, according to Virno, could be interpreted as a reply to Jean-Jacques Rousseau's common will, given that for Marx it was not the will but rather the intellect that producers accumulated; or better yet, an unfolding of the Aristotelian concept of *poietikos* (productive or poetic intellect). Whichever it is, general or common intellect would be the true driving force of the production of wealth, one that calls for alienation. According to Marx, the life of a thinker could be like that of a foreigner. He needs to remove himself from his community and, like a foreigner, should never feel at home. For Virno, this is the situation for so many people nowadays, and not only immigrants or refugees. As the multitude breaks apart, it becomes ever more ambivalent. It converges not in a common will but in a common intellect, that is, in the life of their minds.

Marx (1933, 83) was still analyzing intellectual labor, dividing it into two types. There were activities resulting in merchandise with an existence independent of the product itself (books, paintings, art objects, etc.), but there were also those whose product was inseparable from the act of producing it. This was the same distinction between material production and political action studied by Aristotle: work with and without a body of work. Pianists, ballet dancers, teachers, and orators, Marx said, produced work that resulted in a masterful performance and not in an independent product. Moreover, all language is an activity without a body of work that could generate a product but that existed even without it. This statement also points to the idea that general intellect is nothing other than intellect, the power of thought. Virno investigates whether a political act based on general intellect—that is, not just on will, but on the potential of thought—would be possible. This would be an ensemble of epistemic paradigms, artistic experiences, and conceptual constellations that organize social communication and forms of life.

But even if we can recognize all of these possibilities, there are still ideological and structural limitations. In order to deal with them, it is essential to abandon the *saudosismo* for the homogeneities of the Taylorist era, or any nostalgia for the hierarchies and inevitable subservience to certain patterns of thought that we had already gotten used to centuries ago, for that matter. In the specific case of art, there has been a lot of discussion about the nature of its processes and its modes of research, above all regarding contemporary art. The notions of artwork or product (choreography, plays, installations, books, framed visual pieces) seem to be further and further from what artists intend to make or create, at least in their more traditional formats. Nonetheless, the pressures of the market continue to insist on the organizing parameters of the old assemblages and categories.

Philosophically speaking, the debate has matured somewhat. It is not a coincidence that many authors who discuss immaterial labor depart from proposals whose foundation is grounded in the work of Deleuze and Guattari. One example of this is Elizabeth Grosz, especially her book *Chaos, Territory, Art: Deleuze and the Framing of the Earth* (2008).

Grosz departs from a philosophy in dialogue with feminist theory and ethology, which allows for thinking about relationships that are not exclusively aesthetic and that do not seem to seek any one meaning or chain of meanings, but rather a network of common forces. Grosz recognizes that art produces problems and provocations beyond affect, sensations, and intensities, but they are not necessarily products or pieces of work. What she understands as intensities are the forces of space, time, and the very materials from which the experience is born.

What is important to Grosz in this discussion is an art of affect much more than any kind of representation or univocal image. For Grosz, all forms of art are first and foremost forms of creativity or production of sensations. Spinoza was the one who stressed the importance of affect outside of the understanding of common sense (see chapter 3) as bodily states of mind.

Art would be able to establish, then, a bridge between a living body, the forces of the universe, and the creation of the future. It would also be a strategy to make matter expressive; that is because it regulates and organizes the materials. It emerges when sensation can set itself apart and gain autonomy from both its creator and the one who perceives it. On the line of flight proposed by Deleuze, Grosz identifies art where and when something leaves the chaos whence it came, and can breathe and have its own life, configured as an artistic process.

In this sense, art and nature share a common structure: that of excess and of production that does not have another use apart from producing knowledge, a flow of images, thoughts that spring from the coevolution of body and environment. The first gesture of art, Deleuze said, is not the externalization of one's own strengths to the body and its energies. It is the making of a frame. A cutting out or reshaping of chaos. This is necessarily the organization of a space-time or a plan of composition. In this sense, borders and walls are not just what secure and divide; they can be an interface with the power to create new connections. The wall, like a membrane, is a basis for coexistence; it doesn't need to be univocal and incontrovertible. It is also important to note that not just one kind of frame exists. Each mode of organization represents one way to connect body and environment. The border that inhibits is the border that is impermeable. Others guarantee life. The evolutionary history of these interfaces, as I prefer to call them when thinking about the presence of the body in transit with its surroundings, is also a history of their deterritorialization. That is because every time a relationship is constructed, it is deconstructed. It is a movement of territorialization that, when it marks off a space, is also deterritorialized and provokes a displacement. Territorialization occurs when an environment sets itself apart. The surroundings are no longer random.

Art is also an operator of visibility to the extent that it creates its plans of composition. But it is necessary to point out that it does not activate perceptions alone. Deleuze used to say that the artist, like the philosopher, has a precarious state of health, not due to any specific illness, but because the artist draws something out of life that is always too much for a single person. The artist lives with this silent ability. That is the reason why what philosophy has to offer to art cannot be a new theory of art, but rather a sharing of power over chaos. We might say the same in relation to science. It is not a matter of trying to validate or prove anything, but of making the shared concerns more complex.

The chaos that both Deleuze and Grosz were talking about is not the common-sense definition of lack of order, but rather a condition. Art, science, and philosophy are considered by these authors as three ways of dealing with chaos, and that is why they can meet. As Noë made clear, however, what crosses these three fields of knowledge is, inevitably, the body in motion. It is in this way that thought is organized.

Art from this perspective is not a productive arrangement of qualities, but rather the ability to organize territory. This makes it a local action, but with the power of autonomy and communication in broader contexts. Once again, everything depends on processes of translation. For that to happen, art depends neither on science nor on philosophy. Art is autonomous but keeps in contact by way of its points of departure: chaos, territory, and the body. It is always the gesture that gives power to the image. What it communicates, not only to others but to itself, is a communicability and not a ready-made meaning. All writing is an assemblage of power. Writing the gesture is no exception.

Keeping track of all of these discussions, I propose that at this point, what is presumed to be immateriality (of labor and specifically of art) be rethought beyond the material/immaterial binary. Immaterial labor is not restricted to its own specific medium and its respective action. It destabilizes precisely the means/end or medium/product relationship in favor of an activation of mediations that extrapolate the scope of the action itself, acting on other fronts. The problem is that for many authors this would mean the absence of materiality. What we are dealing with, however, are two different concepts. When we are referring to the body, the absence of a final product does not mean the absence of materiality.

At first glance, this can seem like simply a change of vocabulary. But the recognition that all thinking, and all creative processes in particular, has materiality may come to represent an important step toward new discussions and actions. Paul M. Churchland (1998, 17) explains that the materialist theories of the mind demonstrate how mental processes and states are those of a physical system called the brain that, in turn, only carries out actions because it is incorporated, in the sense of being embodied. Only dualistic theories of the mind allow for thinking of mental states as being different from phenomena of a nonphysical or nonmaterial nature.

So considering the acts of thinking, creating, and knowing to be immaterial phenomena is a way of dislocating them from the body and from its specific contexts, revealing a camouflaged Cartesian point of view that only helps reaffirm assemblages of power, not profane them.

Next, I will present some research about the body's immune system that, in my opinion, adds to the debate, not only in the sense of reaffirming the materiality of the process of cognition, but also in that of proposing the paradigm of immunization as a strategy of political resistance.

## PART III

# Paradigms of Immunization

Even if, right now, my own window is narrow in time and fragmented in its understanding, somewhere, somehow I must say that we'll have to give death back its rights.

(Francisco Varela)

# 5

# Systemic Crises

In January 1824, Virginia Eliza Clemm Poe, the young wife of Edgar Allan Poe, suffered a terrible accident. While she was singing, she began to bleed from her mouth. It was a pulmonary hemorrhage, a symptom of tuberculosis, which at the time was known as "the white plague" and which took her life one month later at the age of only twenty-five (Weiss 2002).

What was poignant about the death of the young singer was the image of blood streaming from her mouth, drowned in music and in the phantasms that arose from that point on. As Susan Sontag explained (1977), two of the illnesses that seem to have generated the most metaphors and phantasms, in all the history of medicine, are tuberculosis and cancer. In some way, even with the causes supposedly detected, the ways that these illnesses transformed themselves into operators of systemic crisis in the body seemed untranslatable.

Indeed, all self-organizational illnesses showed ever-increasing evidence of the complexity of the immunological system. As Francisco Varela (2001) observed—himself a victim of immunological problems resulting from a series of liver diseases—it could no longer be explained as a war between antigens and antibodies as it had been for so long in colleges and medical schools. In recent decades, it has become clear that the nature of bodily identity changes when a syndrome such as AIDS destabilizes an organism, once the immune system makes its cognitive abilities explicit.

Traditionally the immune system had always been understood as something able to protect the body from external attacks. The military metaphors of attack and defense always seemed convincing, relying on a clear separation between the inside and the outside of the body, the self and the Other. As Varela and Anspach (1994, 274–75) explain, however, the cognitive abilities of the immune system gradually became clearer, not only after the appearance of AIDS, but already starting with illnesses like lupus, in which the organism is no longer able to recognize what is from its own body and begins to identify the self as Other, combating it. Many researchers recognize that the immune system is able to learn and remember, creating an autonomous and intelligent network. For Varela, it is only when we recognize the autonomy of this process, in the biological, neural, and immunological networks, that we finally discover how we think with our entire bodies.

In political philosophy, the paradigms of immunization and the notion of autonomous networks have also been widely used to construct critical thinking. Some of the authors who broached the topic were Niklas Luhmann (1984) in his development of systems theory; Donna Haraway (1988), who proposed a discourse of the immune system to address the question of postmodern bodies; Jean Baudrillard (1991), who in order to study "evil" discussed an artificial sterilization compensated by internal immune defenses; and Jacques Derrida (2003), who went on to develop a relationship between immunity on the one hand and trauma and compulsive repetition on the other, especially in his writings after the 9/11 terrorist attack in New York. For these authors, the term *immunity* would tend toward autoimmunity, the nonplace where contemporary politics is made.

In order to understand a bit more about the importance of metaphors of immunization in contemporary politics, it is also worth mentioning the research of Roberto Esposito (2008), which has become increasingly recognized for the relationship it draws between immunity and community. Esposito asks whether this relationship is one of juxtaposition or contrast, or whether it isn't more a matter of being part of a larger movement in which each term is inscribed reciprocally in the logic of the other.

According to Esposito, the relationship between immunity and individual identity emerges when immunity connotes the meaning by which the individual is defended from the expropriating effects of community, protecting those that have the chance to defend themselves from the risk of contact with those that do not. The risk that Esposito refers to is loss of identity, as has already been discussed by Varela and others in the field of neurophilosophy. In political terms, immunity both presupposes community and negates it. That is because, in order to survive, every community is forced to internalize its own opposition, which remains consequently as the means of contrast with being in that community. It is the internalization of immunity, according to Esposito, that forms the basis of modern biopolitics. The modern subject who enjoys political and civil rights represents an attempt to obtain immunity from the contagion of possibly forming part of a community. This attempt at immunizing the individual from that which is common ends up placing the community itself at risk at the same time, as an immunized turn in on itself as well as on its constitutive member.

This is only one among a wide range of other ambivalent points that permeate the ontological and epistemological discussion of identity, subjectivity, and the systemic recognition of the self.

Sovereign power, that topic that Giorgio Agamben has discussed in such depth, acts to immunize the community from its own excess, as is noted in the desire to acquire goods from others, as well as from all of the violence that this relationship implies. That is the reason why, from Esposito's standpoint, the immunity that is in political-juridical language alludes to a temporary or permanent exemption of the subject in relation to concrete obligations or responsibilities that under normal circumstances would link one subject to others. Instead of juxtaposing or imposing an external form that would subject one to the domination of another, the paradigm of immunization (*bios* and *nomos*, life and politics) emerges as two constitutive elements of the same indivisible whole that take on meanings from their interrelationships. It's not just a matter of bringing life and power together. Immunity is the power to preserve life. And no power outside of life exists, just as life is never outside of power relationships.

Without speaking specifically about immunity, Maurizio Lazzarato (2002) has asserted on the topic of community that, in this context, to produce newness or new forms of life is to invent new desires and new beliefs, new associations and forms of cooperation—a prerogative that is not solely that of great geniuses and not exclusive to science or industry, but extends to everyday people as well. From this perspective, subjectivity is not an effect or ethereal superstructure, but rather a living force and a political power. Peter Pál Pelbart (2003) somewhat reiterates this proposal, affirming the potential of common life of the masses as a mix of collective intelligence, reciprocal affection, production of bonds, the capacity to invent new desires and beliefs, new associations, and forms of cooperation. This would be the primordial source of wealth within capitalism itself, which also operates an economy that produces information and is not based solely on either automatic behavior or compartmentalized solitude.

Increasingly, mainstream publications discuss what these communities of thought might be and the possibility of a bond with others and not simply a consumer relationship in the most pejorative sense of the term. It's not easy to understand the formulation of new groupings and the way that paradigms of immunization are reorganized. Jean-Luc Nancy (1990) observes that often where there is society, community is lost. Whoever speaks of society is already speaking of loss or degradation of community intimacy, in such a way that community is the very thing that society destroyed. However, it is important to note that this sense of community that Nancy refers to is not that of the essence of a community or a phantasm that represents communion, unity, or belonging. What is understood is that the loss of those "essential" understandings gives rise to new communities. That is because the notion of community today has heterogeneity, plurality, and, in many cases, distance as its primary condition, as occurs in virtual communities. The desire for unitary fusion presupposes a fictional purity that has led to a number of exclusions in recent years. Praise of unitary fusion and the community of the people was tied to Nazism and other political-religious movements that preached for the death of each of us (and at times, of all of us), only to be reabsorbed into the life of the nation or into a transcendental afterlife. Obviously, such experiences of death could not be considered a basis for communities. The focus has been on conceiving community as the sharing of a separation created by singularity. That means the denial of a relationship between self and self, same and same, and suggests one in which the Other intervenes. This Other is irreducible, introducing the asymmetry that does not allow for all to be reabsorbed into a broader totality. A community can no longer be described as a place of communion or possession. It is always supported by paradoxical relationships.

Thinking about materiality, as studied by authors like Judith Butler and Susan Bordo; and about immateriality, as proposed by Karl Marx, Paolo Virno, Lazzarato, and others; as well as notions of community and immunization, one can understand more clearly how ideas change all the time, depending on the nature we are describing, and the ideal that guides these descriptions.

Three centuries ago, nature, the body, and all worldly phenomena were understood in general as automata, subject to deterministic mathematical laws that were able to predict the future just as they had determined the past. There are still remnants of this kind of thinking, but they were subjected to radical questioning in 1984, when Ilya Prigogine and Isabelle Stengers proposed what became known as the New Alliance, describing a metamorphosis that would renew our conception both of the relationship between humankind and nature and of science as a cultural practice.

One of the important points of this way of thinking is that neither philosophical nor scientific analysis can ever be a monologue. Both researchers explain that there is no shortage of ways that an object under observation can disprove the researcher's hypothesis, regardless of how seductive and plausible the hypothesis may be. In this way, research is always a game of risk, and can also be studied itself as a paradigm of immunization. When scientific analysis discovers questions to which nature responds coherently, or a theoretical language by which countless processes can be deciphered, research creates new territories. They are never predictable a priori, but reflect different choices. In a certain sense, one can say that a choice is an unnecessary orientation before it is taken, but once it happens, it provokes an inexorable transformation in the world in which it took place.

That is why the metamorphosis of scientific knowledge can be understood as starting from the very moment in which the objects of the natural sciences were no longer immutable phenomena and situations were no longer considered stable. People do not want to study what remains the same anymore; rather they want to study what is transformed, such as geological and climatic disturbances, the evolution of species, the origin of and changes in the norms that influence social behavior, or forms of life.

It is practically impossible to guess the behavior of a reality different from ours, not subjected to our beliefs, ambitions, and hopes. It is always a matter of an agreement between theoretical hypotheses and experimental responses. More than a century ago, science abandoned the illusion of theoretical extraterritoriality, including as it pertains to culture. It became urgent for science to start recognizing that it was part of the culture in which it was developed. Without that, Prigogine explains, it would be destined to inevitable atrophy and ossification.

In order to reflect on this contamination among forms of knowledge, Prigogine recognized the "rediscovered time" of a nature made up of multiple and divergent evolutions that leads to the coexistence of times both irreducibly different and articulated. In the eighteenth century, time for Newton was absolute, true, and mathematical in itself, and, by its very nature, it transpired without any relationship to anything outside of it. This Newtonian time could also be called one of duration. Already Henri Bergson's conception of time stated that the universe had a duration, but that the more we delve into the nature of time, the better we understand that duration is an invention, a creation of forms, a continuous elaboration of absolute newness. For Prigogine, from now on, those two dimensions came to be articulated instead of being excluded. Rediscovered time is also a time which no longer speaks of solitude but rather speaks of the alliance between people and the nature they describe.

When Agamben suggested the term "form-of-life" (written as a single term), it was his intention to speak about a life that could not be separated from its form. A life that ultimately could never be isolated as bare life (*zoë*). A life that cannot be separated from its form is a life for which what is at stake in its way of living is, precisely, living. That does not mean that it is somehow "immaterial," or that it is nothing more than a "brutally biological" machine. Life processes are not simply facts but rather possibilities of life, and these cannot be predicted a priori by a set of given concepts.

What characterizes life is movement in its broadest sense, movement that goes much further than any visible displacement, but that coincides with what we call thinking. If Alva Noë is correct in identifying the cognitive nature of the sensorimotor system, as is Varela in recognizing the cognitive nature of the limbic system, what distinguishes bare life from biopolitics is ultimately not a distinction, but a rate of complexity that depends on the possibility of just how many mediations with environment one can create from oneself. What characterizes bare life is not the fact of it being a culturally unqualifiable biological machine, but rather the impossibility of translating its cognitive acts.

Thus the invasion of bare life into the ambit of biopolitics as proposed by Agamben, or the transformation of bare life into biopolitics as observed by Michel Foucault, is not configured as a contradiction when we set aside the nature/culture dichotomy. It is not a matter of identifying life itself or life as culturally qualified, but rather a matter of detecting the impact of the gap, silence, the hole, the impossibility of mediations.

It was Gilles Deleuze and Félix Guattari themselves (1980) who explained how, during their research, they had found two axes: the axis of meaning, and the axis of subjectification. But meaning did not exist without a blank slate on which to inscribe its signs and redundancies. And subjectification did not exist without a black hole where one could accommodate consciousness and passion, and also, of course, their redundancies. The assemblage that was borne out of the crossing of those two axes was nothing more than a face. But this face was not merely an external wrapping that speaks, thinks, and feels. It is as if the face surfaced when we least expected, in the meanderings of falling asleep, a twilight state, a hallucination, or a peculiar physical experience. In these cases, there would be nothing more to explain, nothing to interpret.

A few years prior, in *Anti-Oedipus* (1972), the same two authors had pointed out that civilized modern societies define themselves by the processes of decoding and deterritorialization; and these processes are endless. Each time something is deterritorialized, it is reterritorialized. These neoterritorialities are at once artificial, archaic, and residual. They are a do-it-yourself way of resuscitating ancient codes and, at times, of inventing jargon.

Vladimir Saflate (2008, 203) considers this description to still be relevant and concludes that the "bipolar structure of our life-forms is an astute means of control, given that true control occurs when the blackmail of a forced choice is imposed on us."

It is not easy to deal with this statement. After all, how are these choices expressed? The witness, Agamben explained, is a certain way of bringing the impossibility of speaking to words, and what is left is not what remains, but rather the very gap of what survives at the point of the impossibility of speaking. Thus the gray areas are not just between speech and silence, challenging the limits between body and environment, life and rights, politics and economics, anomie and mourning,[1] public and private life, being on the outside and belonging. In these areas, which I prefer to call destabilization zones, opposites are not mutually exclusive, but render each other indeterminate and point to what really matters. This brings us once again to the beginning of the book and the practice of translation. As I have no intention of repeating what has already been said, I would like to conclude by suggesting a relationship between translation and friendship.

It's no coincidence that recent lists of scholarly publications in political philosophy, philosophy of the mind, and art theory all include discussions of friendship. It is not a matter of sharing common interests, like a kind of prerequisite for affective projects of interpersonal translation. Agamben (2009, 90) explains that in Greek as well as in Latin, there are two terms for otherness: *allos* (*alius*) is generic alterity, and *heteros* (*alter*) is otherness as opposition between two or, in other words, heterogeneity. A friend is not another I, but rather an otherness in sameness: the possibility of becoming other than oneself. Friendship is the desubjectification of the most intimate feeling of self.

In neuroscientific terms, the thing that desubjectifies what is most intimate in us is empathy: the actions of our mirror neurons. Political action is probably what we put into practice when we act out what António Damásio (2003) calls the virtual corporeal loop, that is, the feeling of "as if it were someone else's body." As there is no separation between nature and culture, we cannot imagine that this might be an exclusively biological function, exempt from each and every assemblage of power. The difference lies, first and foremost, in time. The brain can produce modifications of maps of the body in milliseconds, but for a political act to modify its environment, it usually takes a bit longer.

> We can never predict the future of a complex system. The future is open, and this openness applies as equally to small physical systems as to the global system, the universe in which we find ourselves.
>
> (Ilya Prigogine, *The Birth of Time*)

> The only event that each of us can foresee with any certainty is that of one's own death. But if the idea is more or less tolerable it is because, without exception, the hour at which it will arrive remains completely unforeseeable. Unpredictability replaces immortality.
>
> (François Jacob, *Of Flies, Mice, and Men*)

# Notes

## Foreword

1. Her areas of interest, as some of the titles above suggest, include contemporary dance and performance studies from Brazil, Japanese arts and culture, and art and communication. Her education includes a PhD in communication and semiotics from PUC-SP (1997) and postdoctoral degrees from the University of Tokyo (2003), the International Research Center for Japanese Studies (2006), and New York University (2007).

## Translators

1. Cameron Crowe, dir., *Jerry Maguire* (TriStar Pictures, 1996).
2. Friedrich Nietzsche, *Also sprach Zarathustra* (Chemnitz: Ernst Schmeitzner, 1884), 26–27.

## Preface

1. Tavia Nyong'o, *Afro-fabulations: The Queer Drama of Black Life* (New York: New York University Press, 2019).
2. Saidiya Hartman, *Wayward Lives, Beautiful Experiments, Lose Your Mother: A Journey along the Atlantic Slave Route and Scenes of Subjection* (New York: W. W. Norton, 2019).
3. Haraway, Donna, *Manifestly Haraway* (Minneapolis: University of Minnesota Press, 2016).
4. Giorgio Agamben, *Creation and Anarchy: The Work of Art and the Religion of Capitalism*, trans. Adan Kotsko (Stanford, CA: Stanford University Press, 2019).
5. Gilles Deleuze, *L'Abécédaire* (Paris: Éditions Montparnasse, 2004), DVD.

## Chapter 1

1. The term *structuralism* comes from structure (*structura* in Latin) and commences in an architectural sense, the way in which a building is constructed. Between the seventeenth and eighteenth centuries it expanded into an analogy for the living being (the body), the integral parts of a concrete being organized in a totality. From then on, these parts could be structures of anatomy, psychology, geology, mathematics, and so forth. The term *structure* is practically absent in Hegel and barely appears in Karl Marx, being consecrated for the most part in the nineteenth century with Émile Durkheim in *Les règles de la méthode sociologique* (1895).

2. As Terry Eagleton uniquely described it: "Fate pushed Roland Barthes under a Parisian laundry van, and afflicted Michel Foucault with AIDS. It dispatched Lacan, Williams, and Bourdieu, and banished Louis Althusser to a psychiatric hospital for the murder of his wife. It seemed that God was not a structuralist" (2005, 13).

3. Since 1970, research in the field of cognitive science has demonstrated through complex experimental protocols how a great part of our thought is unconscious, but that doesn't necessarily make it repressed or less important (Lakoff and Johnson 1999, 10).

4. Heidegger's discussion on language, silence, and voice is very complex, but anyone not familiar with the topic can best understand it through Agamben's explanations about testimony, especially with regard to the case of *Muselmänner* in Auschwitz. The title of Agamben's book *What Remains of Auschwitz* refers not to what is left, but to an essential gap, to what survives in action, in the impossibility of speaking. Later in this chapter, some questions will be made clearer based on the study of so-called *vita nuda* (bare life).

5. Very little was known in France at the time regarding the work of Charles Sanders Peirce, or the discussions in the area of linguistic philosophy by Ludwig Wittgenstein and John Austin, who underscored the need to think about language in a more complex way (beyond linguistic and semiotic), bridging different possibilities for formulating and recognizing the idea of representation. These sources have reshaped discussions about the body (in the sense of how it represents and translates) that had already surfaced, particularly in Foucault, bringing the logic of discontinuity to other temporal axes, including the most internal axes of the organism (see chapter 3). So the process had already begun a few years before, but it was marked by many discontinuities.

6. In the East, modernity does not correspond to a specific period of time, but rather is usually considered synonymous with the West itself.

7. For Sousa Santos, thinking about roots is thinking about all that is deep, permanent, unique, singular: that which gives us a sense of security and consistency. At its best, it would already be directed toward what is variable, ephemeral, replaceable, possible, and indeterminable. Although such thinking may affirm that it has nothing to do with oppositions, by evoking the differentiation between these terms, it runs the risk of reinvigorating the belief in the existence of roots and other questionable vocabulary such as origins, matrices, and so on.

8. In regard to this, it is worth reading the philosopher Paul M. Churchland's book *Matter and Conscience: A Contemporary Introduction to the Philosophy of Mind* (1988). It was written for students and identifies, in an exceptional and didactically useful way, at least ten modalities of mind/body dualisms, many of them supposedly anti-Cartesian.

9. The becoming that gives direction to Viveiros de Castro is becoming in the Deleuzian sense, inspired by Heraclitus, Greek tragedy, Nietzsche, and Stéphane Mallarmé. It is a process that always implies a metamorphosis: the becoming-animal of people, the becoming-verb of nouns, and so on. Becoming is possible starting from a space of deterritorialization and the linking together of two multiplicities (Sasso and Villani 2003, 101–5).

10. Michal Kobialka also discusses these representations of power in *This Is My Body: Representational Practices in the Early Middle Ages* (2003), in which he makes clear that even at the beginning of the Middle Ages, the concept of the body and of power was dynamic and not static, as it is often identified. When Christ says, "Hoc est corpus meum," at the Last Supper, he gives rise to a process of the metaphoric visibility of the body that stimulates other representational practices of power. But Agamben (2002) also calls attention to how the sovereign body is configured as an indistinct gray area, as it needs to stay outside of the order to ensure its power of decision over the state, even if it is supposedly inside of it.

11. From Clement of Alexandria, the term *oikonomia* merges with the notion of providence and starts to mean the government of the world and the history of humankind. This translates as *dispositio* in Latin, from which *dispositivo* (device, apparatus, or assemblage) derives.

## Chapter 2

1. Oswald de Andrade (1890–1954), author of the *Anthropophagist Manifesto* (1928), took inspiration from the ritual of anthropophagy, a phenomenon found in the Americas among the Aztec, Maya, and Inca that Christopher Columbus described with the phrase "comían los hombres." However, from the beginning it seemed clear that it had nothing to do with eating out of hunger or gluttony, but was rather a ritual to express a way of thinking, a worldview. It was a matter of something that characterized the first phase of humanity, something that meant much more than what the Jesuits and colonizers said it did. The metaphoric operation linked to ritual anthropophagy had one peculiarity, which was its aptitude in transforming taboo into totem, the opposite value into a favorable one; this was nothing more than the very nature of life. The taboo represented the untouchable, the limit, "the Other."

2. Suely Rolnik has broached the subject in a number of articles, but this specific phrase was said during a lecture in the seminar "A Revolta da Carne" (The Revolt of the Flesh), during the exhibition of the same name, which I organized alongside Ricardo Muniz Fernandes and Hideki Matsuka in August 2009 at the Serviço Social do Comér-

cio Consolação in São Paulo (Social Service of Commerce Consolation, an important Brazilian cultural center).

3. What is transmitted genetically are the characteristics that make any living being more adapted to the cultural strategy of survival, or rather, to the ability to create behavior patterns in line with established actions in contact (and in conjunction) with the environment. The genetic evolution of human lineage added the analogous path of cultural evolution, and these two forms of evolution came to be linked together.

4. I was not able to verify this story about Mandela through any other source, but I still decided to keep the example because it is cited in Leach's book and is considered emblematic of the discussion; however, I would like to let readers know that I could not confirm this account.

5. As Nagib (1995) explains, *In the Realm of the Senses* was a film that, despite all of its cultural references, is mostly an attack on Japan. Not because it is pornography, as Japan is the largest producer of pornography in the world, but because it presents sex practiced explicitly and in real time. The actors paid a large price for participating in the project. Eiko Matsuda needed to move to Europe after the film, and Tatsuya Fuji had serious marital problems. Oshima answered to legal processes and lost, turning from then on to international productions.

## Chapter 3

1. As explained earlier, enaction, proposed by Francisco Varela and others, is a critique of classical cognitivism, given that it does not recognize predetermined representations as adequate to the outside world. On the contrary, it has to do with representations that emerge from specific situations.

2. It was Hilary Putnam who used this term *protoconcept*, in works from 1992 and 1999, to address cognitive capacities in animals.

3. Although he may not be familiar with this scientific bibliography, it is Giorgio Agamben who proposes the definition of a gesture as the communication of communicability (2000). This approach will be addressed once again later on.

## Chapter 4

1. Obviously, it is impossible to generalize. Not all experiences represent political movements or actions of resistance. Under the enormous umbrella called contemporary art there is much diversity, including increasingly recurring strategies for creating art as an object of consumption. One of the artists to have discussed this theme is Takashi Murakami, who wrote the manifesto *Superflat*, where he exposes some of the most important questions present in the art-market alliance.

2. The professor Augustin Berque is the translator of Watsuji's work into French, which is actually the only translation into a Western language.

## Chapter 5

1. Anomie is the state of a lack of goals and loss of identity brought on by radical transformations. The term has one of its sources in Émile Durkheim in the book *Suicide* and is repeatedly quoted by Agamben (2004, 2006 2008).

# Bibliography

AGAMBEN, Giorgio. 2002. *Homo Sacer*. Vol 1, *O poder soberano e a vida nua*. Translated by Henrique Burigo. Belo Horizonte: Editora UFMG.

AGAMBEN, Giorgio. 2007. *Profanações*. São Paulo: Boitempo editorial.

COSTA, Jurandir Freire. 2004. *O vestígio e a aura: Corpo e consumismo na moral do espetáculo*. Rio de Janeiro: Editora Garamond.

FOUCAULT, Michel. 1983. *Vigiar e punir*. Petrópolis: Editora Vozes.

FOUCAULT, Michel. (1971) 2002. *A ordem do discurso*. São Paulo: Edições Loyola.

GHIRALDELLI, Paulo, Jr. 2007. *O corpo: Filosofia e educação*. São Paulo: Editora Ática.

GLEISER, Marcelo. 2011. "Stevie Wonder, Lucrécio e o medo." *Folha de S. Paulo*, Caderno Mais!, fev., p. 3.

JOHNSON, Mark. 1987. *The Body in the Mind: The Bodily Basis of Meaning, Imagination, and Reason*. Chicago: University of Chicago Press.

KATZ, Helena, and Christine GREINER. 2001. "Corpo e processo de comunicação." *Revista Fronteiras* 3 (2): 65–74.

LAKOFF, George, and Mark JOHNSON. 1999. *Philosophy in the Flesh: The Embodied Mind and Its Challenge to Western Thought*. New York: Basic Books.

LAKOFF, George, and Mark JOHNSON. 2002. *Metáforas de la vida cotidiana*. São Paulo: Educ/Mercado de Letras.

MATTELARD, Armand. (1994) 1997. *L'Invention de la communication*. Paris: Édition de la Découverte.

NAJMANOVICH, Denise. 2001. *O sujeito encarnado: Questões para pesquisa no/do cotidiano*. Rio de Janeiro: DP&A Editora.

NIETZSCHE, Friedrich. 1998. *Assim falou Zaratustra*. Rio de Janeiro: Editora Bertrand Brasil.

ORTEGA, Francisco. 2002. "Da ascese à bioascese: Ou do corpo submetido à submissão do corpo." In *Imagens de Foucault e Deleuze*, edited by Luiz B. Lacerda Orlandi, Margareth Rago, and Alfredo Veiga-Neto, 139–73. Rio de Janeiro: DP&A.

PELBART, Peter Pál. 2003. *Vida capital: Ensaios de biopolítica*. São Paulo: Editora Iluminuras.

SEBEOK, Thomas. 1991. *The Sign Is Just a Sign*. Bloomington: Indiana University Press.

## Bibliographic Note

The majority of authors and books that appear in the following bibliographic listing are cited in the book. There are exceptions such as some philosophical works and their secondary sources that, although not mentioned, can assist readers in the elaboration of their own research. This is a book written for students, and its objective is to forge pathways and introduce certain questions without the presumption of treating them in an exhaustive way. For that reason, the bibliography is laid out to help in the continuation of these processes. This time around, in contrast to my previous book, I preferred not to separate the references by topic. It seemed more coherent to pull it all together, obeying only the convention of alphabetical order, as usual.

It remains important to state that apart from academic books, many films, performances, poems, art exhibitions, and conversations were essential for the formulation of the itinerary and the choices of study topics, given that the topic of the body in crisis is marked by the combination and disruption of knowledges. Among the international references that marked my work in particular were a few Japanese artists who were part of the Angura Movement, performing in dance, theater, visual arts, literature, and cinema, especially between 1960 and 1980. I will dedicate an important part of the continuation of this research to the new statutes of the body in Japan.

ADORNO, Theodor. 1973. *Negative Dialectics*. Translated by E. B. Ashton. New York: Continuum.

ADORNO, Theodor. (1968) 2008. *Teoria estética*. Lisbon: Edições 70.

AGAMBEN, Giorgio. 1993a. *A comunidade que vem*. Translated by Antônio Guerreiro. Lisbon: Presença.

AGAMBEN, Giorgio. 1993b. *Stanzas: Word and Phantasm in Western Culture*. Translated by Ronald L. Martinez. Minneapolis: University of Minnesota Press.

AGAMBEN, Giorgio. 2000. *Means without End: Notes on Politics*. Translated by Vincenzo Binetti and Cesare Casarino. Minneapolis: University of Minnesota Press.

AGAMBEN, Giorgio. 2002. *Homo sacer*. Vol 1, *O poder soberano e a vida nua*. Translated by Henrique Burigo. Belo Horizonte: Editora UFMG.

AGAMBEN, Giorgio. 2004a. *Homo sacer*. Vol 2, *Estado de exceção*. Translated by António Guerreiro Iraci D. Poleti. São Paulo: Boitempo editorial.

AGAMBEN, Giorgio. 2004b. *The Open*. Translated by Kevin Attell. Stanford, CA: Stanford University Press.

AGAMBEN, Giorgio. 2006. *A linguagem e a morte: Um seminário sobre o lugar da negatividade*. Translated by Henrique Burigo. Belo Horizonte: Editora UFMG.

AGAMBEN, Giorgio. 2007. *Profanações*. Translated by Selvino J. Assmann. São Paulo: Boitempo editorial.

AGAMBEN, Giorgio. 2008. *O que resta de Auschwitz: O arquivo e a testemunha*. Translated by Selvino J. Assmann. São Paulo: Boitempo editorial.

AGAMBEN, Giorgio. 2009. *O que é o contemporâneo? E outros ensaios*. Translated by Vinícius Nicastro Honesko. Chapecó: Unichapecó.

ALTHUSSER, Louis. 1976. "Ideologie et appareils ideologiques d'État." In *Positions, 1964–1975*, 67–125. Paris: Éditions Sociales.

AMÉRY, Jean. (1977) 1980. *At the Mind's Limit: Contemplations by a Survivor of Auschwitz and Its Realities*. Translated by Sidney Rosenfeld and Stella P. Rosenfeld. Bloomington: Indiana University Press.

ARENDT, Hannah. 1963. *Eichmann in Jerusalem: A Report on the Banality of Evil*. New York: Penguin.

ARENDT, Hannah. 1989. *Origens do totalitarismo: Anti-semitismo, imperialismo, totalitarismo*. Translated by Roberto Raposo. São Paulo: Companhia das Letras.

ARENDT, Hannah. 2001. *A Condição Humana*. Translated by Roberto Raposo. Lisbon: Relógio D' Água.

ARIÈS, Philippe. 1974. *Western Attitudes toward Death from the Middle Ages to the Present*. Translated by P. M. Ranum. London: Marion Boyars.

ARISTOTLE. 1984. *The Complete Works of Aristotle*. Edited by Jonathan Barnes. Princeton, NJ: Bollingen.

ARNHEIM, Rudolf. 1969. *Visual Thinking*. Berkeley: University of California Press.

ARTAUD, Antonin. 2004. *Oeuvres Complètes*. Paris: Gallimard.

AUSTIN, John. 1976. *How to Do Things with Words*. Oxford: Oxford University Press.

AYDEDE, Murat, ed. 2005. *Pain: New Essays on Its Nature and the Methodology of Its Study*. London: Bradford Books.

BADIOU, Alain. 2001. *Ethics: An Essay on the Understanding of Evil*. Translated by P. Hallward. New York: Verso.

BARTHES, Roland. 1968. "L'Éffet de réel." In *Communications* 11:84–89.

BARTHES, Roland. 1994. "Sur la théorie." In *Oeuvres complètes*, vol 2. *1968–1971*, edited by Éric Marty. Paris: Seuil.

BATAILLE, Georges. 1954. *L' Expérience intérieure*. Paris: Gallimard.

BATAILLE, Georges. 1957. *L' Erotisme*. Paris: Les Éditions de Minuit.

BATAILLE, Georges. 1970. "L'Abjection et les formes misérables." In *Oeuvres Complètes*, vol. 2, *1922–1940*. Paris: Gallimard.

BATAILLE, Georges. 1979. "Dossier de Lascaux." In *Oeuvres Complètes*, vol. 9. Paris: Gallimard.

BATAILLE, Georges. 1988a. "À propos de récits d'habitants d'Hiroshima." In *Oeuvres Complètes*, vol. 11, 172–87. Paris: Gallimard.

BATAILLE, Georges. 1988b. "La part maudite." In *Oeuvres Complètes*, vol. 1. Paris: Gallimard.

BATAILLE, Georges. 2003. *A História do Olho*. Translated by Eliane Robert Moraes. São Paulo: Editora Iluminuras.

BAUDRILLARD, Jean. 1993. *Symbolic Exchange and Death*. Translated by I. H. Grant. London: Sage.

BAUMAN, Zygmunt. (1989) 1998. *Modernidade e Holocausto*. Translated by Marcus Penchel. Rio de Janeiro: Jorge Zahar Editor.

BAUMAN, Zygmunt. 1999. *Modernidade e ambivalência*. Translated by Marcus Penchel. Rio de Janeiro: Jorge Zahar Editor.

BENJAMIN, Walter. 1978. *Reflections*. Translated by Edmund Jephcott. New York: Schocken.

BERQUE, Augustin. 1993. *Du geste a la citè: Formes urbaines et lien sociale au Japon*. Paris: Gallimard.

BERQUE, Augustin. 2008–9. "Mediance et être vers la vie." *Ebisu-Études Japonaises* 40–41:17–29.

BERTHOZ, Alain. 2001. *Le sens du mouvement*. Paris: Odile Jacob.

BERTHOZ, Alain. 2003. *La Décision*. Paris: Odile Jacob.

BERTHOZ, Alain, and Gerard JORLAND. 2004. *L' Empathie*. Paris: Odile Jacob.

BHABHA, Homi. 2003. *O Local da cultura*. Translated by Myriam Ávila, Eliana L. Reis, and Gláucia R. Gonçalves. Belo Horizonte: Editora UFMG.

BLACK, Joel. 2001. *The Reality Effect: Film Culture and the Graphic Imperative*. New York: Routledge.

BLOOM, Harold. 1994. *The Western Canon*. New York: Harcourt Brace.

BOIS, Yves-Alain, and Rosalind KRAUSS. 1999. *Formless: A User's Guide*. New York: Zone Books.

BORDO, Susan. 1993. *Unbearable Weight: Feminism, Western Culture, and the Body*. Berkeley: University of California Press.

BOURDIEU, Pierre. 1980. *Le Sens pratique*. Paris: Éditions de Minuit.

BUTLER, Judith. 1987. *Subjects of Desire: Hegelian Reflections in Twentieth-Century France*. New York: Columbia University Press.

BUTLER, Judith. 1993. *Bodies That Matter*. New York: Routledge.

BUTLER, Judith. 2006. *Precarious Life: The Powers of Mourning and Violence*. London: Verso.

CAILLOIS, Roger. 1967. *Les jeux et les hommes: Le masque et le vertige*. Paris: Gallimard.

CAMPOS, Haroldo. 1970. *Metalinguagem: Ensaios de teoria e crítica literária*. Petrópolis: Vozes.

CANGUILHEM, George. 1991. *The Normal and the Pathological*. Translated by Carolyn R. Fawcett. New York: Zone Books.

CARROLL, Noel. 1996. *Theorizing the Moving Image*. Cambridge: Cambridge University Press.

CASTRO, Eduardo Viveiros de. 2008. *A inconstância da alma selvagem*. São Paulo: Cosac Naify.

CASTRO, Eduardo Viveiros de. 2009. *Metaphysique cannibales: Lignes d' anthropologie post-structurale*. Paris: Presses Universitaires de France.

CASTRO, Eduardo Viveiros de, and Manuela L. Carneiro da CUNHA. 1986. "Vingança e temporalidade: Os Tupinambás." *Anuário Antropológico* 85:57–78.

CÉLINE, Louis-Ferdinand. 1934. *Journey to the End of the Night*. Translated by John H. P. Marks. Boston: Little Brown.

CHOMSKY, Noam. 2002. *Para entender o poder*. Translated by Eduardo Francisco Alves. Rio de Janeiro: Editora Bertrand Brasil.

CHURCHLAND, Paul. M. (1988) 1998. *Matéria e consciência: Uma introdução contemporânea à filosofia da mente*. Translated by Maria Clara Cescato. São Paulo: UNESP.

CLARK, Andy. 1997. *Being There: Putting Brain, Body, and World Together Again*. Cambridge: Bradford Books.

CLARK, William. 2006. *Sexo e as origens da morte: Como a ciência explica o envelhecimento e o fim da vida*. Translated by Ryta Vinagre. Rio de Janeiro: Record.

CORNELL, Drucilla. 1992. *The Philosophy of the Limit*. New York: Routledge.

DAMÁSIO, António. 1994. *O erro de Descartes: Emoção, razão e o cérebro humano*. Translated by Dora Vicente and Georgina Segurado. São Paulo: Companhia das Letras.

DAMÁSIO, António. 2003. *Em busca de Espinosa: Prazer e dor na ciência dos sentimentos*. Translated by the author. São Paulo: Companhia das Letras.

DARWIN, Charles. 1981. *The Descent of Man, and Selection in Relation to Sex*. Princeton, NJ: Princeton University Press.

DAWKINS, Richard. 1976. *The Selfish Gene*. Oxford: Oxford University Press.

DEAN, Carolyn J. 1992. *The Self and Its Pleasures: Bataille, Lacan and the History of the Decentered Subject*. Ithaca, NY: Cornell University Press.

DEBORD, Guy. 1997. *A Sociedade do Espetáculo*. Translated by Estela dos Santos Abreu. Rio de Janeiro: Contraponto.

DELEUZE, Gilles. 1972. *Gilles et Félix Guattari. Anti-Oedipus, Capitalisme et Schizofrénie*. Paris: Les éditions de Minuit.

DELEUZE, Gilles. (1992) 2005. *Dicionário de Filosofia*. Translated by Bento Prado Jr. and Alberto Alonso Muñoz. São Paulo: Ed. 34.

DELEUZE, Gilles, and Félix GUATTARI. 1980. *Milles Plateaux*. Paris: Les Éditions de Minuit.DERRIDA, Jacques. (1967) 1979. *L'Écriture et la différence*. Paris: Seuil.

DERRIDA, Jacques. 1992. *Donner la mort in L' éthique du don: Jacques Derrida et la pensée du don*. Paris: Metailié-Transition.

DERRIDA, Jacques. 2003. *Filosofia em tempo de terror: Diálogos com Habermas e Derrida*. Translated by Roberto Muggiati. Edited by Giovanna Borradori. Rio de Janeiro: Jorge Zahar Editor.

DEWEY, John. (1934) 1991. *Art as Experience*. Vol. 10 of *Later Works, 1925–1953*. Edited by Jo Ann Boydston. Carbondale: Southern Illinois University Press.

DIDI-HUBERMAN, Georges. 1995. *La ressemblance informe ou le gai savoir visuel selon Georges Bataille*. Paris: Macula.

DOLLIMORE, Jonathan. 2001. *Death, Desire and Loss in Western Culture*. London: Penguin.

DOSSE, François. (1991–92) 2007. *História do estruturalismo*. 2 vols. Translated by Álvaro Cabral. Bauru: Edusc.

DURKHEIM, Émile. (1895) 2009. *As regras do método sociológico*. Translated by Paulo Neves. São Paulo: Martins Fontes.

EAGLETON, Terry. 2005. *O fim da teoria: Um olhar sobre os Estudos Culturais e o pós-modernismo*. Translated by Maria Lucia de Oliveira. Rio de Janeiro: Civilização Brasileira.

EDELMAN, Gerald. 2001. *Consciousness How Matter became Imagination*. New York: Penguin Books.

ELKINS, James. 1999. *Pictures of the Body: Pain and Metamorphosis*. Stanford, CA: Stanford University Press.

ERLICH, Paul. 2000. *Human Natures: Genes, Cultures and the Human Prospect*. New York: Penguin Books.

ESPINOSA, Baruch. 2008. *Ética*. Translated by Thomas Tadeu. Belo Horizonte: Autêntica.

ESPOSITO, Roberto. 2008. *Bios: Biopolitics and Philosophy*. Minneapolis: University of Minnesota Press.

FOSTER, Hal. 1996. *The Return of the Real: The Avant-Garde at the End of the Century*. Cambridge: MIT Press.

FOUCAULT, Michel. 1971. *Hommage à Jean Hyppolite*. Paris: Presses Universitaires de France.

FOUCAULT, Michel. 1977. *Vigiar e Punir: História da violência nas prisões*. Translated by Ligia Ponde Vassallo. Petrópolis: Vozes.

FOUCAULT, Michel. 1994–98. *Dits et Écrits*. Vols 1 and 2. Paris: Gallimard.

FOUCAULT, Michel. 2004. *Microfísica do Poder*. Translated by Roberto Machado. São Paulo: Graal.

FOUCAULT, Michel. 2006. *A História da Sexualidade*. Vol 1, *A Vontade de Saber*. Translated by Maria Thereza da Costa Albuquerque and J. A. Guilhon Albuquerque. São Paulo: Graal.

FOUCAULT, Michel. (1966) 2007. *As palavras e as coisas*. São Paulo: Martins Fontes.

FOUCAULT, Michel. 2008. *Arqueologia do Saber*. São Paulo: Forense Universitária.

FOUCAULT, Michel. (1966) 2009. *Le Corps utopique: Les Hétérotopies*. Paris: Lignes.

FREUD, Sigmund. 1953–74. *The Complete Psychological Works of Sigmund Freud*. London: Hogarth Press.

GALLESE, Vittorio. 2001. "The 'Shared Manifold' Hypothesis: From Mirror Neurons to Empathy." *Journal of Consciousness Studies* 8 (5–7): 33–50.

GALLESE, Vittorio, and Alvin GOLDMAN. 1998. "Mirror Neurons and the Simulation Theory of Mind-Reading." *Trends in Cognitive Sciences* 2 (12): 493–501.

GARBER, Marjorie. 1997. "Out of Joint." In *The Body in Parts: Fantasies of Corporeality in Early Modern Europe*, edited by David Hillman and Carla Mazzio, 23–51. New York: Routledge.

GAZZANIGA, Michael S. 2005. *The Ethical Brain*. New York: Dana Press.

GIBSON, James J. 1966. *The Senses Considered as Perceptual Systems*. Boston: Houghton-Mifflin.

GREIMAS, Algirdas Julien. 1987. *De l' Imperfection*. Périgueux: Fanlac.

GREINER, Christine. 2005. *O Corpo: Pistas para estudos indisciplinares*. São Paulo: Annablume.

GROSZ, Elizabeth. 2008. *Chaos, Territory, Art: Deleuze and the Framing of Earth*. New York: Columbia University Press.

GUNJI, Masakatsu. 1985. *Buyo: The Classical Dance*. New York: Weatherhill.

HARAWAY, Donna. (1988) 1999. "The Cyborg Manifesto." In *The Cultural Studies Reader*, 2nd ed., edited by Simon During, 271–91. New York: Routledge.

HAUSER, Marc. 1996. *The Evolution of Communication*. Cambridge: MIT Press.

HAUSER, Marc. 2006. *Moral Minds: How Nature Designed Our Universal Sense of Right and Wrong*. New York: HarperCollins.

HEGEL, Georg Wilhelm Friedrich. 1977. *Phenomenology of Spirit*. Oxford: Oxford University Press. In Portuguese: *Fenomenologia do espírito*. 2 vols. Petrópolis: Vozes.

HEIDEGGER, Martin. 2006. *O Ser e o tempo*. Translated by Márcia Sá Cavalcanti Shuback. São Paulo: Vozes.

HELMHOLTZ, Hermann von. 1962. *Treatise on Physiological Optics*. Translated by James P. C. Southall. New York: Dover.

HERCOLES, Rosa Maria. 2005. "Formas de Comunicação do Corpo: Novas cartas sobre a dança." PhD dissertation, Pontifícia Universidade Católica de São Paulo.

HURLEY, Susan. 2003. "Animal Action in the Space of Reasons." *Mind and Language* 18 (3): 231–57.

HUSSERL, Edmund. 1989. "Material Things in Their Relation to Aesthetic Body." In *Ideas Pertaining to a Pure Phenomenology and a Phenomenological Philosophy*, book 2, *Studies in the Phenomenology of Constitution*, translated by Richard Rojcewicz and André Schuwer, 60–95. Dordrecht: Kluwer.

JACOB, François. 1998. *O rato: A mosca e o homem*. Translated by Maria de Macedo Soares Guimarães. São Paulo: Cia das Letras.

JAMES, William. (1890) 1950. *The Principles of Psychology*. 2 vols. New York: Dover.

JANET, Pierre. 1935. *Les débuts de l' intelligence*. Paris: Flammarion.

JOHNSON, Mark. 2008. *The Meaning of the Body: Aesthetics of Human Understanding*. Chicago: University of Chicago Press.

KANT, Immanuel. 1790. *Crítica do julgamento*.

KANT, Immanuel. 2005. *Crítica da razão prática*. Translated by Paulo Barrera. São Paulo: Ícone.

KANT, Immanuel. 2007. *A Crítica da razão pura*. Translated by Lucimar A. C. Anselmi and Fulvio Lubisco. São Paulo: Ícone.

KOBIALKA, Michal. 2003a. "Delírio da carne: Arte e biopolítica no espaço do agora." In *Leituras da Morte*, edited by Christine Greiner and Claudia Amorim, 53–77. São Paulo: Annablume.

KOBIALKA, Michal. 2003b. *This Is My Body: Representational Practices in the Early Middle Ages*. Ann Arbor: University of Michigan Press.

KRACAUER, Siegfried. 1997. *Theory of Film: The Redemption of Physical Reality*. Princeton, NJ: Princeton University Press.

KRISTEVA, Julia. 1982. *The Powers of Horror: An Essay on Abjection*. Translated by Leon S. Roudiez. New York: Columbia University Press.

KRISTEVA, Julia. 1988. *Étrangers à nous-mêmes*. Paris: Fayard.

KURIYAMA, Shigehisa. 1999. *The Expressiveness of the Body and the Divergence of Greek and Chinese Medicine*. New York: Zone Books.

LACAN, Jacques. (1970) 1971. *Écrits*. 2 vols. Paris: Seuil.

LACAN, Jacques. 1998. *Seminar XX*. New York: Norton.

LANDOWSKI, Eric. (1997) 2002. *Presenças do outro: Ensaios de sociossemiótica*. Translated by Mary Amazonas Leite de Barros. São Paulo: Perspectiva.

LAZZARATO, Maurizio. 2002. *Puissance de l' invention: La psychologie économique de Gabriel Tarde contre l' économie politique*. Paris: Les Empêcheur de penser en ronde.

LAZZARATO, Maurizio, and Antonio NEGRI. 2002. *Trabalho Imaterial: Formas de vida e produção de subjetividade*. Translated by Mônica Jesus. São Paulo: DP&A.

LEPECKI, André, ed. 2004. *On the Presence of the Body: Essays on Dance and Performance Theory*. New York: Routledge.

LEVI, Primo. 1958. *Se questo è un uomo*. Rome: Giulio Einaudi.

LEVI, Primo. 1997. *A Trégua*. São Paulo: Companhia das Letras.

LEVI, Primo. 2004. *Os afogados e os sobreviventes*. São Paulo: Paz e Terra.

LEVINAS, Emmanuel. 1969. *Totality and Infinity: An Essay on Exteriority*. Translated by Alphonso Lingis. Pittsburgh, PA: Duquesne University Press.

LEVINAS, Emmanuel. 1985. *Ethics and Infinity*. Translated by Richard A. Cohen. Pittsburgh, PA: Duquesne University Press.

LAKOFF, George, and Mark JOHNSON. 1980. *Metaphors We Live By*. Chicago: University of Chicago Press.

LAKOFF, George, and Mark JOHNSON. 1999. *Philosophy in the Flesh*. New York: Basic Books.

LEACH, Neil. 2006. *Camouflage*. Cambridge, MIT Press.

LÉVI-STRAUSS, Claude. 1952. *Les structures élementaires de la parenté*. Paris: De Gruyter.

LÉVI-STRAUSS, Claude. 1958. *Anthopologie structurale*. Paris: Plon.

LLINÁS, Rodolfo. 2002. *I of the Vortex: From Neurons to Self*. London: Bradford Books.

LOPARIC, Zeljko. 2006. *Heidegger*. Rio de Janeiro: Jorge Zahar Editor.

LUHMANN, Niklas. 1984. *Social Systems*. Stanford, CA: Stanford University Press.

LUMSDEN, Charles J., and Edward O. WILSON. (1979) 2005. *Genes, Mind and Culture: The Coevolution Process*. New York: World Scientific.

MARGULIES, Ivone, ed. 2003. *Rites of Realism: Essays on Corporeal Cinema*. Durham, NC: Duke University Press.

MARTÍN-BARBERO, Jesús. 2007. *La educación desde la comunicación*. Bogotá: Grupo Editorial Norma.

MARX, Karl. (1858) 1982. *Elementos fundamentais para a crítica da economia política*. Translated by José Barata-Moura. Lisbon: Edições Progresso.

MAUSS, Marcel. (1936) 1968. "Les techniques du corps." In *Sociologie et Anthropologie*, 4th ed., 364–86. Paris: Presses Universitaires de France.

MAUSS, Marcel. 1968. "Essai sur le sacrifice." In *Oeuvres*, vol. 1, *Les fonctions sociales du sacré*. Paris: Minuit.

MELBERG, Arne. 1995. *Theories of Mimesis*. Cambridge: Cambridge University Press.

MERLEAU-PONTY, Maurice. 1945. *Phénoménologie de la perception*. Paris: Gallimard.

MERLEAU-PONTY, Maurice. 1964. *Le visible et l'invisible*. Paris: Gallimard.

MURRAY, Timothy, ed. 1997. *Mimesis, Masochism, and Mime: The Politics of Theatricality in Contemporary French Thought*. Ann Arbor: University of Michigan Press.

NAGIB, Lucia. 1995. *Nascido das cinzas: Autor e sujeito nos filmes de Oshima*. São Paulo: Edusp.

NAGIB, Lucia. 2006. "Materialismo corporeso." In *Leituras do sexo*, edited by Christine Greiner and Claudia Amorim. São Paulo: Annablume.

NANCY, Jean-Luc. 1990. *La Communauté desouvrée*. Paris: Christian Bourgois.

NEGRI, Antonio. 2001. *Exílio: Seguido de Valor e Afeto*. Translated by Renata Cordeiro. São Paulo: Editora Iluminuras.

NEGRI, Antonio. 2003. *5 lições sobre o império*. Translated by Alba Olmi. Rio de Janeiro: DP&A Editora.

NEGRI, Antonio, and Michael HARDT. 2005. *Multidão: Guerra e democracia na era do império*. Translated by Clovis Marques. Rio de Janeiro: Record.

NIETZSCHE, Friedrich. 2006. *O Nascimento da tragédia ou Helenismo e Pessimismo*. Translated by J. Guinsburg. São Paulo: Companhia das Letras.

NOË, Alva. 2004. *Action in Perception*. Cambridge: MIT Press.

OPHIR, Adi. 2005. *The Order of Evils: Toward an Ontology of Morals*. New York: Zone Books.

PATRAKA, Vivian. 1999. *Spectacular Suffering: Theater, Fascism, and the Holocaust*. Bloomington: Indiana University Press.

PEIRCE, Charles Sanders. 1935–66. *Collected Papers of Charles Sanders Peirce*. Edited by Charles Hartshorne, Paul Weiss, and Arthur W. Burks. Cambridge, MA: Harvard University Press.

PELBART, Peter Pál. 2003. *Vida capital: Ensaios de biopolítica*. São Paulo: Editora Iluminuras.

PIAGET, Jean. 1952. *The Origins of Intelligence in Children*. New York: Basic Books.

PIAGET, Jean. 1971. *Biology and Knowledge*. Chicago: University of Chicago Press.

PINKER, Steven. 2007. *Do que é feito o pensamento: A língua como janela para a natureza humana*. Translated by Fernanda Ravagnani. São Paulo: Companhia das Letras.

PRIGOGINE, Ilya. 1991. *O Nascimento do Tempo*. Translated by João Gama. Rio de Janeiro: Edições 70.

PRIGOGINE, Ilya, and Isabelle STENGERS. 1984. *A Nova Aliança*. Translated by Miguel Faria and Maria Joaquina Machado Trincheira. Brasilia: Universidade de Brasilia.

RIZZOLATTI, Giacomo, and M. A. ARBIB. 1998. "From Monkey-like Action Recognition to Human Language: An Evolutionary Framework for Neurolinguistics (with commentaries and author's response). *Behavioral and Brain Sciences* 28:105–67.

RIZZOLATTI, Giacomo, and Corrado SINIGAGLIA. 2006. *Lãs neuronas espejo: Los mecanismos de la empatia emocional*. Translated by Bernardo Moreno Carrillo. Barcelona: Paidós.

ROACH, Joseph. 1996. *Cities of the Dead: Circum-Atlantic Performance*. New York: Columbia University Press.

RORTY, Amélie. 1991. Mind in Action: Essays in the Philosophy of Mind. Ohio: Beacon.

SAFLATE, Vladimir. 2008 *Cinismo e falência da crítica*. São Paulo: Boitempo editorial.

SASSO, Robert, and Arnaud VILLANI, eds. 2003. *Le vocabulaire de Gilles Deleuze*. Paris: Centre de Recherches d' Histoire des Idees.

SAUSSURE, Ferdinand. 1916. *Cours de linguistique générale*. Paris: Loose Leaf.

SCARRY, Elaine. 1985. *The Body in Pain: The Making and Unmaking of the World*. New York: Oxford University Press.

SHEETS-JOHNSTONE, Maxine. 1994. *The Roots of Power: Animate Form and Gendered Bodies*. Chicago: Open Court.

SHERRINGTON, C. S. 1918. "Observations on the Sensual Role of the Proprioceptive Nerve-Supply of Extrinsic Ocular Muscles." *Brain* 41:332–42.

SLOTERDIJK, Peter. (1983) 1987. *Critique of Cynical Reason*. Translated by Michael Eldred. Minneapolis: University of Minnesota Press.

SLOTERDIJK, Peter. 1993. *No mesmo barco: Ensaio sobre a hiperpolítica*. Translated by Claudia Cavalcanti. São Paulo: Estação Liberdade.

SLOTERDIJK, Peter. 1999. *Regras para o parque humano: Uma resposta à carta de Heidegger sobre o humanismo*. Translated by José Oscar de Almeida Marques. São Paulo: Estação Liberdade.

SLOTERDIJK, Peter. 2002a. *A mobilização infinita para uma crítica da cinética política*. Translated by Paulo Osório de Castro. Lisbon: Relógio D'Água.

SLOTERDIJK, Peter. 2002b. *O desprezo das massas: Ensaio sobre as lutas culturais na sociedade moderna*. Translated by Claudia Cavalcanti. São Paulo: Estação Liberdade.

SONTAG, Susan. 1977. *Illness as Metaphor*. New York: Farrar, Straus and Giroux.

SOUSA SANTOS, Boaventura de. 2000. *A crítica da razão indolente: Contra o desperdício da experiência*. São Paulo: Cortcz.

SOUSA SANTOS, Boaventura de. 2002. *Introdução à uma ciência pós-moderna*. Porto: Afrontamento.

SOUSA SANTOS, Boaventura de. 2006. *A gramática do tempo*. São Paulo: Cortez.

TAUSSIG, Michael. 1993. *Mimesis and Alterity*. London: Routledge.

TODOROV, Tzvetan. 1989. "Crimes against Humanities." *New Republic*, July 3, 1989, 28–30.

VARELA, Francisco. 2001. "Intimate Distances: Fragments for a Phenomenology of Organ Transplantation." In *Journal of Consciousness Studies* 8 (5–7): 259–71.

VARELA, Francisco, Evan THOMPSON, and Eleanor ROSCH. (1991) 1993. *L' Inscription Corporelle de l' Esprit 1991: Science cognitives et expérience humaine*. Translated by Vêronique Havelange. Paris: Seuil.

VARELA, Francisco, and Mark R. ANSPACH. 1994. " The Body Thinks: The Immune System in the Process of Somatic Individuation." In *Materialities of Communication*, edited by Hans Ulrich Gumbrecht and K. Ludwig Pfeiffer, 273–85. Stanford University Press.

VERNANT, Jean-Pierre. 1985. *La mort dans les yeux*. Paris: Hachette.

VIRILIO, Paul. 2002. *Ground Zero*. Translated by C. Turner. New York: Verso.

VIRILIO, Paul. 2003. *Art and Fear*. Translated by Julie Rose. New York: Continuum.

VIRNO, Paolo. 2004. *A Grammar of the Multitude: For an Analysis of Contemporary Forms of Life*. Translated by Isabella Bertoletti, James Cascaito, and Andréa Casson. New York: Semiotext(e).

VIRNO, Paolo, and Michael HARDT. 1996. *Radical Thought in Italy: A Potential Politics*. Minneapolis: University of Minnesota Press.

WATSUJI, Tetsurô. 2005. *Fûdo*. Translated by Augustin Berque. Manuscript in author's possession.

WEISS, Allan S. 2002. *Breathless: Sound Recording, Disembodiment, and the Transformation of Lyrical Nostalgia*. Middletown, CT: Wesleyan University Press.

WELTON, Donn. 1998. *Body and Flesh: A Philosophical Reader*. Oxford: Blackwell.

WILSON, Robert. 1999. *The MIT Encyclopedia of the Cognitive Sciences*. Cambridge: MIT Press.

WITTGENSTEIN, Ludwig. (1953) 2009. *Philosophical Investigations*. New York: Wiley-Blackwell.

ŽIŽEK, Slavoj. 1999. *The Ticklish Subject: The Absent Centre of Political Ontology*. New York: Verso.

ŽIŽEK, Slavoj. 2003. *The Puppet and the Dwarf: The Perverse Core of Christianity*. Cambridge: MIT Press.

ŽIŽEK, Slavoj. 2004. *Organs without Bodies: On Deleuze and Consequences*. New York: Routledge.

ŽIŽEK, Slavoj, and Daly GLYN. 2006. *Arriscar o impossível: Conversas com Žižek*. Translated by Vera Ribeiro. São Paulo: Martins Fontes.